To Robert,

Your, your family and your restaurants are great!

I wish you a Happy, Healthy New Year.

Hope you enjoy my story.

Paul Lane

Continued Praise for *The Courage to Go On*

"Paul is a pioneer of entertainment licensing. He has lived an amazing life and his story has many life lessons. An incredible entrepreneur and executive but an even better human being. A great read."

—Brad Globe, former head of Licensing and Marketing for Steven Spielberg's Amblin Entertainment

"Paul Lane's thought provoking insights into life's complications are eye opening. Get set for an exciting excursion of memories, challenges, and imagination. Lane's debut book is a must-read."

—Janice Grossman, former Publisher, *New York Magazine*

"Paul's book is well-written in such a way that it keeps you engrossed and wanting to know what has happened next. I have spent thirty plus years on the board of the American Film Institute and have read numerous scripts, seen many films and read quite a few books. This book can take its place with the ones I felt were very good. Lane's story is one that tells of one man's trials and tribulations and how he dealt with them over the course of his life."

—Lawrence Herbert, American Film Institute board member

"Paul Lane was one of the premier apparel executives I have ever had the privilege to work with. He ran a large company with great success and understood and managed well the idiosyncrasies of the entertainment licensing business. I am so impressed with this book! His writing is captivating, poignant, and gripping. He is both sensitive and

articulate and I felt like I was there with him through all of the highs and lows of his incredible life."

—Dan Romanelli, founder of Warner Bros Studio Stores and Warner Bros Consumer Products; spearheaded licensing campaigns including Looney Tunes, Space Jam, Batman, Superman, Scooby Doo, and Harry Potter

"Paul Lane was the first licensee to come onboard for Strawberry Shortcake. The concept was presented to him with lots of promises but not a single doll had been shipped. In other words, no one knew of this concept. Paul came onboard immediately and became one of our best licensees. He was intuitive and enthusiastic. He is a great visionary and more important, he knew how to sell. After Strawberry, he was the first to take Care Bears and numerous other properties. Thanks again Paul for all your talent and initiative."

—Carole MacGillvray, Former President of MAD (Marketing and Design), A General Mills Toy Group (Developer of Strawberry Shortcake and Care Bear Properties)

"Themes like family, tragedy, love, and disappointment really drive the humanity of who Paul is and what defines him. One chapter after the next is filled with twists and turns and the plot continues to develop. Everyone loves a person who loves hard and that emanates radiantly from these pages. I truly applaud Paul for doing this as it leaves behind his legacy, and in his own words, which is invaluable. As Paul says, we all have our own story, and I am honored to have seen what a remarkable life he has lived."

—Alana Zonan, Director of Video Productions, "Industrial Color"

"Paul Lane's writing is crisp, professional, humble, funny, and above all, real. Every moment along the way, I feel that I am experience everything side-by-side with you, whether it's wearing pajamas in the sleeping quarters, or missing Joan, or nearly getting stabbed to death by the crazed inmate on the psychiatric unit. You have succeeded mightily."
—Michael Levin, *New York Times* bestselling author
and renowned ghostwriter

"A poignant and extremely moving memoir an an inspirational journey. Beautifully written. A personal history that will touch my heart forever."
—Luana

The Courage to Go On:
It's Called Life

The Courage to Go On:
It's Called Life

A Memoir by

As Told to Shannon McDermott

Redwood Publishing, LLC

ISBN: 978-1-947341-76-0 (hardcover)
ISBN: 978-1-947341-77-7 (paperback)
ISBN: 978-1-947341-78-4 (e-book)

Library of Congress Catalogue Number: 2019914469

Published & Designed by Redwood Publishing, LLC (Orange County, California)
Interior Design: Ghislain Viau
Cover Design: Michelle Manley

First Printing. Printed in the United States of America

10 9 8 7 6 5 4 3 2 1

Dedicated to my sister Rita.
She would have loved this book.

Table of Contents

Foreword
Written by Shannon McDermott

I'VE ALWAYS SUBSCRIBED TO THE BELIEF THAT everyone has a story that is capable of inspiring folks while breaking a heart or two along the way. That stranger who sits across from you on the subway or the person who kindly holds the door for you is most likely harboring grief and doing their best to keep going. After spending a great deal of time with Paul, I realized however, that gut-wrenching tragedy has a tendency to follow some of us more than others.

Biographic narratives are my favorite to create, so when the opportunity popped up to help Paul share his story, I jumped on it. Initially, this project was based around the tale of how a poor kid from Flatbush, Brooklyn, took whatever scraps life gave him and turned them into opportunities. As an '80s baby, I was excited to hear the behind-the-scenes stories of how Paul worked with the creators of classics like *The Strawberry Shortcake Movie,*

Who Framed Roger Rabbit, and *Barney's Great Adventure* to bring these iconic characters to life. His scrappy story of ascending to the executive level could intrigue everyone from a savvy CEO to someone who is inspired by a good rags-to-riches tale.

But the direction of the narrative began to shift as Paul and I grew closer throughout the project, and he began to share with me the tragedies of his personal life. Death has been an unfortunate constant in this man's life, and devastating scenarios have shaped much of the direction it has taken.

As trust grew, so did the depth of Paul's sharing. And through our conversations, we determined that sixteen powerful stories stitched together into an anthology would be the best way to tell Paul's unique, devastating, and ultimately inspiring story. Consider this as more of a *Greatest Hits* album as opposed to a traditional, chapter-by-chapter memoir.

I've grown to love many things about Paul, but one of my favorites is his absolute lack of tolerance for hyperbole. He may joke around and act overconfident to the point of cocky, but at his core, he is truly modest. This book is by no means the typical self-aggrandizing bore that some memoirs turn into. It is simply a story about a man who wanted to share the story of his wins, losses, and everything in between.

Perhaps you're like me, curious about the traits of wildly successful people as you wonder whether or not you, too, will ever become someone great. If that's you, then you are definitely reading the right book. If you're looking to sharpen your business savvy, read this book. If you're looking to hop on an emotional roller coaster and ride through a lifetime of triumph and tragedy, read this book. If you're curious about what true love actually looks like, read this book. I feel grateful to know Paul, and I feel strongly that he is someone everyone should know.

Before you dive into the tale of Paul Lane, I will leave you with one story that perfectly sums him up. One weekday morning at 9:00 a.m., we were wrapping up another one of our FaceTime work sessions (we both work best at dawn), and Paul stopped me as I was wrapping up the call.

"Is everything all right with you?" he asked, and, surprising both of us, I burst into tears. A foolish man had decided to break my heart the night before, and I guess the fresh grief was plastered across my face.

"Can I tell you tomorrow? I don't want to cry for an hour," I begged him, thoroughly embarrassed that I was crying over a stupid boy to a man who had endured more tragedy than most folks I've ever met in real life.

"Cry," he instructed me. "Cry so you can get on the other side of whatever it is. Is it about a guy?"

I nodded, feeling even more embarrassed about the fact that I was crumbling over something so silly and predictable.

"Well, let's hear it. What happened?"

"It's so stupid," I replied. "It's nothing really. I'll be over it by this afternoon."

"Bullshit," he retorted. "You always listen to me. For once, let me listen to you."

And for the next twenty minutes, I shared my thirty-something-year-old dating woes with my eighty-six-year-old pal as he listened intently and offered an old-school dude's perspective. Our experiences working on this book together would make for a great movie.

The thing about Paul is that you have to do a bit of work to get inside his heart, but once you're in, he cares about you relentlessly. I am truly grateful for the chance to help Paul share his life's stories with you. I hope you enjoy reading this book as we enjoyed writing it.

Chapter 1

Dad

LIFE AS I KNEW IT BEGAN ON THE EVENING OF October 6, 1945. I was thirteen years old, sleeping soundly in a single bed in the tiny room I shared with my older sister, Rita. The unmistakable screams of my mother found their way into my dreams and forced me awake. As consciousness took over, I realized these screams were, in fact, real. I instinctively shot to my feet and walked out of my bedroom to investigate. As I drifted down the short hallway toward my parents' room, my mother's screams got louder, and I began hearing murmurs of voices I didn't recognize. My sleepy eyes slowly adjusted to the light, and I saw nurses and police officers in uniform, huddled around my parents' bed. The screams and strange voices melted together into a hum as my eyes narrowed in on the face of my father, who was lying there unconscious. He was eerily peaceful, still, and unresponsive to the chaos that surrounded him. This glimpse of him lasted no more than a couple of seconds, and the next thing I saw was the white sheet being pulled over his head. My father was gone.

The day of my father's funeral came shortly after his passing. It was an exhausting and surreal day full of pandemonium caused by devastated friends and family. As I stood in the synagogue surrounded by adults crying, fainting, and screaming his name, all I could think was, *My God, my father's body is in that box.* This wasn't the type of reality a thirteen-year-old boy is meant to process. I vividly remember looking around in amazement and in a daze, as concerned adults took turns doing their best to comfort me or shoving smelling salts in my face, to stop me from fainting. I was nowhere near fainting, just bewildered by the frenzy of despair that surrounded me and the fear of what my life was about to be like without my father around.

"Julius! *JULIUS!*" several folks screamed as they entered the room that housed my father's casket. I don't remember ever feeling more alone in a room packed with people. The service came to an end and, one by one, friends and family walked to their cars and formed a funeral procession that led to Wellwood Cemetery in Long Island, where my father was to be buried.

As our large black limousine pulled into the parking lot of Wellwood Cemetery, I noticed two rabbis arguing outside in broad daylight. I pressed the side of my head against the inside of the car window to hear what they were saying without making myself obvious and was dismayed by the realization that their argument was merely a scuffle over which one of them would say the prayers as my father was being lowered into the ground. It wasn't as if they knew him personally and were fighting for the honor of doing it; they were fighting to be paid for the job, which I heard, in those days, was just three dollars. To me, this seemed like a needless dispute that could have been solved in private. However, there they were in the middle of the parking lot, making no effort to conceal their conflict from my father's devastated friends and family. In this singular moment, I found myself reconsidering the entire notion of religion as a whole.

Was it really just about the money?

The scuffle came to an end, but I remained in the car until I heard a loud knock on the window and saw a family friend gesturing to me to come out and join the rest of my father's friends and family around the hole that had been dug in the cemetery lawn.

It was time for the final goodbye.

The victorious rabbi read the prayers with obviously feigned compassion, and sounds of sobs and shrieks rippled through the large crowd as my father was lowered into his grave.

* * *

As a kid growing up, I had no grasp of the concept of poverty. We weren't poor—we lived the same lives as everyone around us. My parents, Rita, and I lived in a modest apartment on Linden Boulevard in Flatbush, Brooklyn, a New York neighborhood that was home to a seemingly homogenized collection of blue-collar families. My father was a factory worker, our next-door neighbor was a bus driver, and I was unconcerned with adult things like survival and what it meant to provide for a family.

My father was the best dad on the block—when he felt like it. But he was also a man who would throw his dinner plate at the ceiling if he didn't like the taste of the food. He was an angry man who yelled a lot, and we were on the wrong side as recipients of his perpetual aggression. My sister hated him, but I always loved him. Since my mother seemed permanently indifferent to my existence, I always thought that at least when my father was angry, threatening, or sometimes slapping me, he was paying attention to me. His cruelty to me was evidence that he cared, while my mother seemed to do everything she could to act like I didn't exist. Perhaps even my young mind understood that the opposite of love is not hatred, but indifference.

My mother and father when they were young.

This angry streak was by no means confined to our family household. During World War II, my father was an air raid warden in our neighborhood, tasked with ensuring that people returned to their homes at the first screech of the sirens that sounded during emergency drills. A few of the neighborhood kids were feeling brave during one of the drills and disregarded my father's commands to go inside. My father promptly approached one of these brave boys, took him by his neck, and head-butted him squarely in the face, his helmet knocking a handful of the boy's teeth out. He was that capable of mayhem.

Me with my father.

Once in a while, my father's spirit and generosity managed to peek through his brutal exterior. He loved the opera and would listen to his music every Saturday afternoon. I remember we had to remain completely quiet so that he could enjoy his favorites. During the holidays, he would always ensure that we had a mountain of presents to open. He loved a celebration and any opportunity to showcase his generosity, and no matter how much I remember the bellowing sound of my father's angry fits, I've never forgotten his excitement over watching us kids open the gifts he gave us. Hours before I watched a nurse pull that white sheet over my father's lifeless body, he had proudly presented me with an album that would hold and showcase my prized stamp collection—I still have it to this day.

Although the cause of my father's death was a heart attack, he was always healthy, energetic, and boisterous. His ability to swing from every rafter, doorway, and scaffolding was reminiscent of an Olympic gymnast, and even to this day, whenever I mention him, I instinctively look upward. My bar mitzvah took place four weeks before my father's passing. It was a happy occasion, and my father was the energetic showman I knew and loved. He stepped on my foot when we danced the hora, then whispered in my ear that it was good luck and that he would dance at my wedding.

As much as he enjoyed my bar mitzvah, my father was not a rich man, and relied on the gifts I received to cover the expenses. Near the end of the night, he escorted me into the bathroom and emptied all of the envelopes I had received throughout as gifts. My take from the evening wound up being around $600, which went straight to the caterer. *Mazel tov indeed*, I thought, as I shuffled away and waited by the door in hopes of getting the traditional gift of a fancy fountain pen most boys receive for this occasion. I never got one.

* * *

During the days that followed my father's funeral, I was nothing more than a detached observer. Our house became a circus of family and friends visiting, bringing food, and driving us all crazy. My dad was always well dressed, and following his death friends, neighbors, and family pillaged his closet … the ties, shirts, and suits my father cherished were snatched up in exchange for a couple

6

of dollars. It was reminiscent of the tragic scene from *Zorba the Greek*, in which friends and family pillaged the dead woman's closet without respect for her memory.

My mother's brother would also visit frequently, even though they never really got along. He would slip me a couple of dollars, and I hated it. I hated it because I needed it, and was in no position to turn it away, and I hated it because it was humiliating.

My dad was a proud man, and in those days, there was a true sense of manhood in being the provider. My resentment of being the recipient of charity would stay with me for the rest of my life, and I never wanted anything I didn't earn. Perhaps this was the beginning of my drive to remain self-sufficient, but all I knew was that during this difficult time and for years to come, I hated charity and I hated that I needed it.

On April 13, 1946—just a few short months after my father died—I woke up to a scene that was as familiar as it was terrifying. The ambulance was parked in our driveway and there was a flurry of nurses and uniformed police officers scattered throughout our tiny apartment.

I ran out of my bedroom just in time to see first responders carrying my wailing mother from our home into the ambulance, and my Uncle Jack getting into his car and following the ambulance down Linden Boulevard. My sister and I sat silently, in shock from a scene that was far too reminiscent of the devastating night we lost our father. A short time later, Uncle Jack returned to collect my sister and me, take us to his home in Queens, New York, and then he jumped back into his car to return to the hospital. The shock of it all rendered me speechless, and all I thought about was that I was about to lose my mother.

Later that evening, Uncle Jack returned and quietly entered the bedroom I was sharing with my sister. He sat at the edge of the bed Rita was sleeping on and began reassuring her that everything was going to be okay.

"Your mother is fine and in good health," he whispered, without the slightest clue that I was awake. He continued to follow up with an update that I was utterly unprepared for:

"SHE DELIVERED THE BABY."

I was overcome with shock, curiosity, and utter confusion. *Baby?* I thought as I lay there still, faking sleep so that my uncle would continue sharing the details of the bombshell he just dropped, and my young mind worked overtime as I began piecing together the situation. My mother's obesity enabled her to hide this pregnancy from the world. Her screams of "What am I gonna do?!" as my father's dead body was being carried out of the home were the cries of an anxious pregnant woman losing her only breadwinner. These cries of agony signaled the realization that she would slip into poverty just as she was about to give birth to a third mouth that would need feeding. As my uncle continued to share every detail with Rita in the darkness of our bedroom, unbeknownst to him I was now wide awake with my eyes closed, processing every word as well as my thirteen-year-old brain was able to. I learned that thankfully, my mother was in good health following the delivery, but my baby sister had been put up for adoption before any of us could change my mother's mind, let alone meet the baby.

As I began to understand what had happened, a new fear washed over me. I knew we were facing hard times after my dad died, and I began to wonder, *Was I next?!* Would I also end up being given up for adoption like my baby sister just was, because I was an added expense my mother could no longer afford? In that moment, I decided I would never breathe a word about the fact that I knew this secret, and hoped with all my heart that I would never be the next one to go.

Rita and I returned home from Queens a few days later to no sign of a newborn. My baby sister would remain a dark family secret that wouldn't surface until almost thirty years after she was born. The shock of it all quickly faded, and my priority became my survival. My adolescent mind had reasoned that if we were poor enough for my mother to give up my sister, I would be next unless I found a way to carry my weight.

My father's death and the adoption of my baby sister provided me with the stark realization that I needed to learn to provide for myself. I canvassed the neighborhood for work and picked up any odd jobs I could find. I worked at the local drug store as well as at a deli around the corner, and I found a part-time job helping out at an appetizing store, a Jewish market that sold what is best described as *the food you eat with bagels*. I learned how to slice smoked salmon from a guy who was missing the tips of his fingers. In those days there were no computers or calculators. I would tally up the totals by hand on the outside of the brown paper bag that would soon hold the purchases. Through this exercise, I developed a quickness with numbers I would rely on for years to come, and through these brief experiences, I started to feel the beginning of my confidence.

Years later, a shrink would tell me that in a mere month, I had transformed from a bar mitzvah boy into the man of the house, and essentially had become an adult overnight. The loss was overwhelming and life changing, but in a weird twist of fate, it forced me to grow up before my time, thrusting me into the school of life. I considered myself lucky to have faced such tragedy, because I developed a sense of independence based on fear and the early realization that my survival was only up to me. Through devastation, I learned that I possessed the courage to go on, and this relentless pursuit of self-sufficiency would follow me for the rest of my life.

Chapter 2

Teenager

HAVE YOU EVER NOTICED THAT TRUE MAGIC TENDS to occur on the heels of tragedy? When I think back on my life, I realize that I always seemed to be wildly lucky amid and in spite of my misfortune. My legendary kinship with my sister Rita remains the greatest gift tragedy ever brought me. Very soon after my father passed away, an unspoken agreement between us came about; we silently declared a truce and decided to take on the world together. It also didn't hurt that my sister had moved out of the bedroom we shared and into my mom's room after Dad passed, quelling the incessant fights we had over closet space and other common annoyances. I was a young man with a bedroom of my own and a beautiful sister who had my back. Things were starting to look up!

By this time, I was a sophomore at Erasmus Hall on Flatbush Avenue. Our family had begun living in our new normal, without my dad. My mom worked in a factory, my sister modeled occasionally, and I worked at the neighborhood appetizing store. I didn't mind working there, but continued to keep my eyes peeled for bigger opportunities. I found out the men's clothing store across the street from my school needed some help, and I convinced them to give me a shot. It quickly became obvious that they needed me to work more, and I knew I needed the money, so I came up with a plan: I would pitch a reduced school schedule—consisting of only core classes—to my principal, Dr. McNeil, and explain to him that I needed more time to work and bring home money. He allowed it on the condition that I keep my grades up. To this day, I am grateful for him and other visionaries who are able to see the benefit of unconventional thinking from time to time.

During the week, I attended class from 8:00 a.m. until noon, and worked at the men's clothing store from 3:00 p.m. until 10:00 p.m. I used the hours in between for homework or to meet one of the neighborhood girls and neck at her parents' house while they were at work. The girls liked me, and I liked them. On Saturdays I worked from 10:00 a.m. until 6:00 p.m., and some Sundays I would work the brunch shift at the Hotel Delmonico on Park Avenue. My friend's dad was the chef there, and we would get paid a couple of dollars a shift to replenish food for the hotel's brunch buffet. All things considered, I was bringing home about thirty dollars a week, which wasn't bad, considering our rent was thirty-six dollars. I discovered confidence through earning money, as it liberated my family from the humiliation, shame, and embarrassment of having to wait for handouts. These feelings ultimately became the basis for many of the decisions I made throughout my life.

The fact that my father left my mother with nothing but mouths to feed forced her to join the workforce. She did so, diligently, and found herself in a factory in the heart of 34th

Street, steaming women's hats over a block form. While I was proud of her, I hated that she worked there and wanted to get her out. The conditions were terrible, and she was working long hours performing laborious tasks in sweltering conditions. This image stayed with me for years to come, and when I had factories of my own, I created the working environment I wish my mother could have had. I wouldn't have hung around the place so much if it weren't for this cute, busty bookkeeper whom I was certain (in my fifteen-year-old mind) was flirting with me. What can I say; she kept me interested in visiting my mom!

My mother's preoccupation with my sister and finding a new husband took up most of her time, and I remained relatively unnoticed. I loved it. As a high school kid in Brooklyn, nothing is sweeter than freedom. I came and went as I pleased and managed to keep up quite a social life between school and work. My best friends and I called ourselves the P.A.C.K., which stood for Paul, Allen, Chick, and Kenny. We also had a friend named Myles, but he didn't really fit into the acronym. A couple of us found our way into Mu Sigma, the local fraternity that afforded me social status, access to girls, and a flashy black-and-gold sweatshirt—Mu Sigma's official colors. I spent quite a bit of time hanging out in front of Garfield's Cafeteria on Flatbush Avenue, wearing that sweatshirt with black pants, my black hair slicked back, and a cigarette dangling from my mouth.

No matter how much I grew into my identity, I was still widely known as "Rita's brother," if you asked most people. I was fine with it; Rita was a star. Some families had businesses; others had cool cars. Our household commodity was my sister's looks. The boys loved her, and the girls wanted to be her. She was never one of those mean beauties, but rather kind and loving, and everyone who knew her thought of her as their best friend. My relationship with Rita was my introduction to unconditional love; she wanted to see me succeed at every stage of my life and supported me every step of the way. Even when I was an awkward, pimply-faced kid in my dusty bar mitzvah suit, Rita made me feel like this handsome guy who could take over the world. This is why I never resented her or felt any jealousy. This is why I didn't bat an eye when I saw the money I contributed from my paychecks go toward outfits for her.

Rita was everyone's pride and joy, and she loved everyone right back. She was our family's hope for making it out of poverty, and we were all counting the days until she either married one of the wealthy men who seemed to knock perpetually on our door or became a movie star. She eventually decided on Marty, a wealthy man who let me drive his Buick Roadmaster and could provide Rita with the elegant life we all wanted for her. I proudly walked her down the aisle on the day of her wedding, a bittersweet day filled with joy for Rita and the grim realization that she was moving to Great Neck with her new husband and it was just my mom and me left in that house. Thankfully, we rarely crossed paths.

I kept up my grades and work schedule, but was gaining more interest in the social side of life. I could always tell a joke, and I've never been one to keep my opinions to myself. One Saturday night, a girl from my cousin Alan's neighborhood threw a party, and I got invited to join everyone in awkwardly hovering around the pretzel bowl as Dean Martin and Frank Sinatra took turns on the record player. I was enjoying my drink of choice at the time—a drop of rye mixed into a cup full of ginger ale—when in walked the girl who would soon become the love of my life.

Joan Weldon was one of those magnets. Much like my sister, she was a stunning woman who also managed to be warm and kind at every opportunity. As soon as I saw her that night at that party, I knew I wanted to spend my time with her. I made my move and lucky for me, she gave me a shot at her heart. I can still hear Nat King Cole's "Fascination" play, as I remember dancing with her that night at the party and falling madly in love soon after.

In the weeks and months that followed, I wasn't much more than a boy in love. When I wasn't at work, I would take the trolley from my home at Linden and Nostrand to her house, which was at Bedford and Avenue Y—almost an hour each way. She was from an upper-middle-class Jewish family, and her dad had a painting business. Her parents weren't thrilled about the idea of me, a boy from the rougher part of town with a widowed working mother and no evident future. She was beautiful, which meant her parents assumed she could do much better than me. I was inclined to agree, but that only made me put more effort in. They were also worried that she would lose her virtue with me, which in those days, in the Jewish faith, was meant to be maintained until marriage. Also, in those days, much simpler pleasures brought the most joy. We would hide in the back room of her parents' house, lie on the floor, and press our fully clothed bodies together—it was ecstasy. The passion and curiosity gave me such a rush, and I couldn't get enough.

I graduated from high school in June of 1950 and felt on top of the world. My graduation took place at the Brooklyn Academy of Music, and my mom and sister showed up for the occasion. My mom even took us for Chinese food afterward, and I remember getting a combination dinner for fifty cents. It was the first time I ever had Chinese food, and one of the few memories of my mom showing up for me. This was also the beginning of my lifelong addiction to Chinese food.

My headshot from high school.

I was excited and anxious about finishing high school. I knew I wanted to marry Joan, and my ever-present tenacity had become driven by my desire to build a life for us—at that point I never told her I wanted to marry her; it was just a fantasy. Joan's parents continued to try to keep us apart, even shipping her off to college upstate, but we were too in love and determined, and her parents' efforts were never successful. The only problem was it was in the middle of the Korean War draft, and guys my age were having trouble getting hired. No one wanted to waste their time training new employees like us if there was a chance we could get drafted into the war at any time. Joan's dad kept offering me a job with him, but I still held on tightly to my pride, and hated the idea of a handout. I also knew I didn't want to spend my days painting houses. I continued my pattern of cobbling a life together through numerous jobs in the hopes of figuring out a way to give my lady the life she deserved. I even gave post-secondary education a shot and enrolled in a business program at Brooklyn College. I didn't last past the first year.

With the draft looming over my head, I was living in a constant state of uncertainty. We were all getting notices of draft, and it was just a matter of time before they got me. On June 3, 1952—two months shy of my twentieth birthday—Allen, Chick, Kenny, Miles, and I were all called to active duty. Thinking of myself as resourceful, I attempted to defer my draft by making the claim that I was my mother's main provider and source of financial stability, and I would need to stay back to care for her. She was called to testify but was quickly deemed self-sufficient and able to care for herself—she was far too young and pretty. My role as an active member of the United States Army was solidified, and in no time, I was kissing Joan goodbye through tears and heading to Virginia to train for a war I likely would not return from.

Chapter 3

730 Days

I ENTERED THE ARMY TERRIFIED. I HAD NO IDEA WHAT was really going on in Korea; all I knew was it was a violent war and thousands of our guys had already lost their lives. Even though my three best friends and I got drafted at the same time, we weren't on the same bus out. I knew a few of the guys in my group from the neighborhood but was relatively on my own.

It was June 3, 1952, when I reported to Fort Dix in New Jersey. I was randomly assigned to the medical corps and became excited at the prospect of becoming a doctor or a medical technician; boy, was I naïve. I was then shipped off to Camp Pickett, Virginia, to begin eight weeks of infantry training followed by another eight weeks of medical training. A feeling of pride for the task at hand quickly replaced my fear, and I was all in.

Camp Pickett was a sharp turn from my life in Brooklyn, sharing a home with women. We slept in quarters that were a long room of bunk beds, no walls, and no sense of privacy. Force of habit had me changing from my soldier uniform into proper pajamas at night, even though all of the other guys would strip down to their shorts and a T-shirt. I looked at all of them and thought they were crazy, but soon realized how absurd I must have looked, being the only one in full-length pajamas. I've always been one to read the room and respond accordingly, so I quickly began sleeping in my shorts and a T-shirt like everyone else. If I was going to stand out, I wanted it to be for some sort of achievement, and not because of my modesty and coordinated night outfits.

Two of the only photos I have from my time in the military.

The food was vile. We called it SOS: *shit on a shingle.* Thankfully, I eventually got hungry enough that it tasted delicious; it's amazing how humans really can adapt to anything. The bathroom situation was the ultimate dismantling of my modesty. Coming from a female-dominated household to an army barracks continued to shock me into my new reality, and I forced myself to quickly get comfortable with showering with other guys and using a bathroom that could facilitate up to thirty men simultaneously in an open space. It was awkward to say the least, but facilitated a quick camaraderie among us.

Infantry training was rough and rigorous. Within a couple of weeks, I reached peak physical condition. I was six feet two, 180 pounds, and could drop down and give one hundred push-ups in the blink of a sergeant's eye. This world was brand new to me, as I was never much of an athlete growing up. I was hanging out with the girls while the guys were on the field. Everything about my army training was an adjustment.

The most powerful aspect of being at Camp Pickett was the truly equalizing experience we all had. Each soldier was from a different background and walk of life, but when we stripped down, had our hair shaped into the standard crew cut, and put the uniform on, we were all the same rank with the same job to do. Two of the guys in my training camp were sons of senators, while a handful of others were farmers. But background didn't matter when we were facing the imminent threat of going up against the North Koreans. To this day, I am firm in my belief that every young person should have this experience, if for nothing else but the sake of building character.

The bunk next to mine was occupied by Jerry Adler. He came from a prominent show business family and seemed more uncomfortable than any of us at the thought of being away from home and his girlfriend. The second morning we had lineup and roll call, and Jerry was missing. He couldn't take being away from his girlfriend any longer, so he went AWOL and snuck back to New York City. I felt for him as I missed my Joan terribly, so when they called his name, I turned my face slightly away from the sergeant, and in as different of a voice as I could muster on the spot, I uttered "Present!" on Jerry's behalf. The commanding officers were none the wiser, and Jerry returned a couple days later without consequence.

Soon after, Jerry was transferred to Governors Island as part of the unit that organized entertainment for the troops. Jerry served his required 730 days in the army and was then discharged. After his service, Jerry continued on in show business and never looked back. He became a stage manager for various Broadway productions. Decades later in Manhattan, I would run into Jerry after I attended *My Fair Lady*, for which he was the stage manager. He remembered me, and we regaled each other with stories of where our paths led following the time we spent in the military. Intrigued by his world, I wound up investing in *Fun City*, a Broadway play he was producing starring Joan Rivers. It was a thrill to be involved with a major production and to learn about what goes into making a show a success. We opened in D.C.; however, the show ended up flopping and closed after two nights. It was quite an expensive lesson to learn, but I enjoyed it nonetheless.

Back at Camp Pickett, I wasn't always the savviest of wingmen as I was when I covered for Jerry's absence. During one of our night maneuvers, I was assigned the position of squad leader, and led my team on an exercise into the Virginia woods on a simulated rescue mission. "This way!" I exclaimed to my men, confidently following the arrow of my compass, which, at the time, I was holding the wrong way. It was dark and visibility was limited, but I trusted my instincts and embraced the opportunity to demonstrate my leadership skills. Those "skills" had me lead my men straight into a muddy ditch twelve-feet deep in the pitch black, causing mass pandemonium. We were a bunch of twenty-year-olds trained for killing and warfare, but you should have seen us all screaming and calling for help—utterly terrified at the thought of bugs and snakes. We collected ourselves, and guys began hoisting each other up and over the ledge of the ditch, then turning back to pull the remaining ones up to ground level. Although it was only a training exercise, I was embarrassed to the core and felt like I had completely let my team down as squad leader.

I also discovered my knack for recognizing opportunities at Camp Pickett. One of the sergeants informed me that each weekend, he drove from the base to Richmond, Virginia, and he had room in his car for four people. He wanted to fill those seats and charge twenty bucks a head, and I seemed to be the best candidate to spread the word. I knew it wouldn't be a challenge, as Richmond was a major destination for soldiers on a weekend pass, either for partying or to connect with transportation to get to their hometowns. From that day forward, I would bring him eighty dollars and four passengers. I never took a cut of the money, but I also quickly realized that I would never have an issue obtaining weekend passes for myself whenever I needed them.

The second part of my training was focused on my assignment to the medical corps. I learned everything from dealing with gunshot wounds to rescuing guys in the field with a stretcher while carrying a medical pack. This part of the training was the most gut-wrenching, as the threat of being killed moments after we would arrive in Korea was made evident. Combat medics weren't allowed to carry weapons and wore a red cross on our helmet as a marker, but we were warned constantly that this meant nothing to the Koreans. The life expectancy for a soldier in active combat at the time was nine minutes, but for the combat medics it was eight. It was a very strange and surreal awareness that your own death was imminent, but somehow, we all accepted it and walked with a sense of pride and readiness.

The worst part of it all was my longing for Joan. I was a hopeless romantic, which softened the brutalities of what I was experiencing around me and ultimately preparing for. She visited me as often as she could, but I realized soon after the draft that I wanted to solidify our union. The looming reality of not returning from Korea caused me to assume that we had a limited future together, and I wanted to spend that time as husband and wife. I also wanted to make sure she received the standard $10,000 that was being issued to the families of soldiers killed in combat. In my mind, death was as sure as my love for Joan, and I wanted to do right by her.

I got permission from Joan's father to marry her and received an advanced pass for the weekend of August 30—this would become our official wedding date. On the morning of August 29, I went through an intense and exhausting training session, crawling through the military training course as live machine gun fire flew over my head. By that evening I had made it back to Brooklyn, fresh off the barracks and doing the best I could to get myself into wedding mode. Joan's father arranged for a beautiful ceremony and reception to be held at the legendary Tavern on the Green in Central Park. It was a whirlwind of happiness and love, and for that weekend, I forgot about my looming deployment and imminent death. I got the girl. I was happy.

Joan's uncle had gifted us a suite for the night at the Waldorf Astoria in Manhattan, where we spent our wedding night. After a clumsy night that was inevitable for two kids unsuccessfully trying to figure things out, I headed back to Virginia with a fellow soldier, his wife, and Joan in tow. When I got back to the base, the commanding officers were kind enough to offer me the only guest quarters on the base that had a private bathroom for my new wife and me to stay in. That was until a higher-ranking officer needed the room for himself, and Joan and I had to stay in one of the wooden barracks with a broken screen, sharing a bathroom with other guests. It wasn't ideal, but we were together and happy. Joan would continue to visit me, and I always managed to secure a weekend pass.

I was a married man now, which gave me all the motivation in the world to serve with pride and do right by my new family. In a blink, my sixteen weeks of training was complete. I was prepared for battle but frightened to death at the thought of never returning. Being hyperaware of your own mortality is a strange way to live, but somehow, I managed to eagerly continue down this path.

Although I had good relationships with the commanding officers, I never once asked for special treatment or a way out. To this day, I couldn't tell why I got so lucky, but out of the two hundred men that got deployed to North Korea out of Camp Pickett, I was one of ten assigned to the Brook Army Medical Center at Fort Sam in San Antonio. I was grateful for the delay in my deployment, but the truth was it could still happen at any given moment.

I reported to Fort Sam after a ten-day break following my training, which I spent with my new wife on an impromptu honeymoon in Florida. Upon my arrival, I was asked to submit my choice of what I wanted to specialize in. I scrolled through the long list of medical specialties and landed on neuropsychiatric technician. *Fancy!* I thought, as I pictured myself in an office with a notepad, jotting down the thoughts and feelings of troubled soldiers as they lay on a couch across from me. I also thought that perhaps there was a chance I would be deployed to the major hospital nearest to the front lines—which was in Tokyo—if I specialized in mental health care as opposed to emergency medical treatment. They granted me my choice and I spent the next two months in classes, learning everything I could about psychoanalysis and the various mental health disorders of troubled young veterans. I also learned jiujitsu—which seemed odd at the time, but I went with it.

I'll never forget my first day on the ward. Armed with my newly acquired background in neuropsychiatry, I was ready to take on the challenge of solving complex mental health issues in my freshly pressed, stark-white uniform. I used a key to open the heavy doors of the locked ward and entered the brightly lit sterile room, eager to get started. I noticed a patient in a barber's chair in the far corner, getting a haircut from an orderly. I walked over to introduce myself and initiate small talk, when in the blink of an eye, the patient had elbowed the orderly out of the way, snatched his scissors, and tackled me to the ground, screaming. He was now on top of me, ready to stab, clutching the scissors inches from my face. As four other orderlies took him off of me, my need for jiujitsu training made complete sense. I learned quickly that my original vision of my playing the role of Sigmund Freud would not be my reality here. I was meant to be the muscle, maintaining as much order as I could in a ward full of soldiers and young veterans who had been trained to kill but were cursed with mental health issues that would ultimately become a major threat to the public. Maintaining some semblance of order amidst this violent mayhem was the crux of my role as a neuropsychiatric nurse.

As always, I became quickly accustomed to my environment.

I had the advantage of being a big guy, and was able to subdue a patient and quickly get him into a straitjacket if need be. I would sit with patients as they received shock therapy one by one, and then walk them back to their room a different, subdued version of themselves. In training, we were expressly told not to hit any of the patients under any circumstances, but sometimes a quick jab or elbow would be the only productive way to get their attention. As removed as some of these guys were from reality, they always understood and reacted to force. It may not have been the most ethical approach, but it got results and kept the nurses and me safe.

Thankfully, my Joan moved down to San Antonio to be with me. We lived in a basement apartment close to the base, eating mayonnaise sandwiches and enjoying our version of the newlywed life. It wasn't ideal, but we were together. I felt like my life was as much of adulthood as I would experience before I was inevitably killed in North Korea. Standard service in the army is two years—730 days—and although I counted down each day with the hope of returning home, the imminent threat of deployment, combat, and ultimately death was ever present.

Joan didn't stay in San Antonio long. She was a Brooklyn girl, and the quiet southern life was not for her. Soon after she left San Antonio, I was given new orders to report to the 101st Airborne at Camp Breckinridge in Kentucky. To this day, the 101st Airborne remains one of the most distinguished operations in the United States military. I proudly reported for duty at the base hospital and was assigned to a psych ward that housed soldiers who experienced such mental turmoil that they never made it out of training. Suicide prevention was my main task, and I learned quickly how important it was to deny these men proper silverware, a belt for their pajamas, and anything else that could be turned into a weapon or a tool for committing suicide.

My time in the 101st Airborne is my proudest era in the army. I kept my colleagues safe amidst violent and unusually difficult and stressed patients, whom I managed to keep alive in spite of their best efforts.

One afternoon, one of our manic-depressive patients was eerily calm as he approached me to have what any untrained person would deem a normal conversation.

"Where ya from, Lane?" he calmly inquired, as if we were two new friends just trying to get to know each other. I answered his questions politely, but his calm demeanor troubled me. I remember from my clinical training in San Antonio that the biggest red flag a manic-depressive person can give is an overly calm demeanor, and I was to consider these moments as the eye of an impending storm. Following this logic, I decided to check on him again, and arrived at his room at the moment he was stringing a sheet over the rafters and preparing to take his own life.

One of our patients used to wander the halls holding an imaginary leash attached to an imaginary dog. During my training, I learned the importance of picking my battles with our patients in order to maintain as much peace as possible—both in their minds and in our ward—so I would indulge him and greet his dog each time we crossed paths. By chance, he found an unlocked door, escaped from our facility, and ran right to the nurses' quarters located only a few hundred feet away from the hospital. As scary as it must have been to have an escaped patient arrive on their doorstep, these nurses were quick on their feet and calmly welcomed him in for milk and cookies, as one of them alerted the police and hospital security. The patient returned to our ward without incident, and shared stories with the other patients of this magical place just beyond the hospital doors that had milk, cookies, and scantily clad women who take excellent care of their visitors. Some of the other patients salivated over his every word, and escape attempts spiked.

Soon enough, another patient managed to escape, and I ended up chasing him through the Kentucky forest. We were both exhausted when I caught up to him and tackled him just before we got to the road, where military police were driving back and forth searching for the escapee. Who knows what would have happened to him or the civilians he could have encountered if I didn't snag him, but fortunately, I was able to get him back to his quarters safely and without incident. Given the circumstances, the assumption was that I'd saved his life. The army took notice of my efforts, and I was promoted to corporal amidst the mass promotion freeze at the time.

I continued to make my way through my 730 days of service, anxious at the thought of waking up one day and being shipped off to Korea. After the Korean War Armistice Agreement was signed on July 27, 1953, the threat of imminent death in combat lessened; however, there was still a chance I could be sent over to help as needed. I was also still fighting against violent and unpredictable guys on a daily basis at the hospital. There never seemed to be any rhyme or reason for the army's decisions surrounding deployment, so we all just carried on with our duties and daily lives, hoping to avoid it.

I was down to just a few days left in my service and was shipped to Fort Lee—this time to be discharged. I was one of the lucky ones. I had made it through my time in the army successfully and could leave with pride and a rare promotion under my belt. But I was terrified, more so than I had been when I was drafted. I was a twenty-two-year-old kid with nothing to my name except for the $238 the army had given me upon discharge. I was heading back to Brooklyn with no job prospects, no car, no home of my own, and a limited education. I also had a wife who was five months pregnant. The fear of getting killed in combat was replaced with the anxiety of becoming a husband, father, and working man. I found myself facing a seemingly insurmountable challenge.

Chapter 4

The Beginning

I LEFT THE ARMY A TERRIFIED TWENTY-TWO-YEAR-OLD father-to-be. During the weeks leading up to my discharge, I remember sitting around the camp with fellow comrades serving their final months, discussing our impending releases. I was anxious and concerned about my ability to care and provide for my family, and if someone had offered me a contract for life for $5,000 a year, I would have happily signed it. While I was glad to be out of the service, I was exceptionally nervous about life going forward.

I got back to Brooklyn on June 3, 1954. That same afternoon, I returned to the neighborhood I grew up in to see my friends and get the word out that I was back and looking for work. One of the neighborhood kids told me his father worked at a small company that manufactured children's apparel in the city, and they had an opening for a shipping clerk in their warehouse. I immediately jumped on the opportunity, and a few days later I was sitting in the tiny office they had at 88 University Place with the owner, Bernie

31

Schwartz. After I shared my brief work history before getting drafted, my willingness to work hard, and my need for a job, he gave me a chance.

My career in clothing manufacturing began in a tiny stock room, where I earned fifty dollars per week folding clothes and preparing merchandise for shipping. Upon hiring me, Mr. Schwartz also offered me the chance to go out and sell if I had the time after completing my packing duties. I saw this as a great opportunity to grow and earn more, and I was eager to take him up on it. I was also comfortable in the basement apartment on Bedford Avenue that Joan and I had moved into upon my return.

Mr. Schwartz assigned me the first product to sell: a baby onesie with a little button fashioned on the chest; the button made a beeping noise when pressed. I brought samples around to major retailers like Macy's, Robert Hall, and Bloomingdales, doing my best to get in front of the buyers. I had the advantage of being a young guy with a pregnant wife, as eager to please as I was to sell. I was never deterred by rejection and continued to shop the product until I finally began to get orders.

I realized my passion for sales quickly, and focused on learning as much as I could about merchandising and strategy. Mr. Schwartz noticed my ability and desire to grow and allowed me to continue to go out in the field. I was getting good reception from the buyers and began to bring in consistent business. My focus then shifted, and I started selling during the day and fulfilling my duties as a shipping clerk at night.

I had been working for Squirt Togs for a little over two months when my first son, Jeffrey, was born. I found myself beginning to thrive in the field, and the company was rewarding my efforts through increases in salary and stature. I had essentially graduated from my packaging job to focus on sales full-time. I remained in a constant state of eager learning, absorbing as much as I could and building my skills as a merchandiser. I also really enjoyed the job and had fun with the product, and Mr. Schwartz definitely got a kick out of the fact that I was a young guy with such great passion.

I had natural instincts for merchandising and started acting on them, while continuing to grow in both salary and stature. I continued to bring in business consistently, and Mr. Schwartz showed his appreciation in the form of bonuses and raises. One particular day, Mr. Schwartz made the well-intentioned yet fatal mistake of sharing his plans to include me in his will. He told me that in recognition of my contributions to his company, I would receive five percent of the business should anything happen to him. From that moment on, every time I would colloquially ask Mr. Schwartz how he was doing, and his response was fine, I couldn't help but feel a tiny bit frustrated, and my future seemed dimmer by the day. And while it was a gesture of kindness, I started to feel trapped, tied down to a company that wasn't mine, and a seemingly limited career. This was the seed that sparked my desire for something more … something of my own.

One Sunday afternoon, I saw an ad in the paper for homes in a new development, in Bellmore, Long Island, for $13,000. I happened to be out with Joan in a borrowed car, and we decided to drive to the southern tip of Long Island just to see what was available. My motivation to provide for my young family was great, and I saw this as a real shot at building a good life. Upon our arrival, there was quite a lineup to view the model home on display. The deal was good, and the neighborhood offered an ideal atmosphere for young families. Since the neighborhood was still in development, they required only a nominal deposit to acquire one of the homes. Joan and I combined the cash we had in our pockets at the time and eagerly left the $100 deposit to secure our spot on Florence Court. The idea of moving into our new house was exciting and gave us something to look forward to. Five months later, our home was built, and I moved Jeffrey, Joan, and Bobo—a Chihuahua we got for one dollar on a trip to Mexico while I was in the service—to our new home and ultimately a better life.

I quickly embraced life as a suburbanite, cutting the lawn and mingling with the other young families who filled the neighborhood; we got along with our neighbors famously. Soon after we bought the house, Joan became pregnant with our second son, Curtis. Life was good.

By now, I was earning $20,000 a year and had a team of salesman and secretaries under me. Retailers all over the city knew me, and Mr. Schwartz kept having to buy more and more sewing machines to keep up with the orders I was bringing in. I had taken the company from $200,000 in sales to over a million, and the company itself had grown exponentially.

My efforts continued to be recognized and I was developing a good reputation in the industry. Perhaps it was a genuine show of appreciation, or a tactic to keep me tied to the company, but as a thank-you, Mr. Schwartz gifted me a 1959 Bonneville and $2,000 cash. *Wow!* It was a few years earlier that I was coming out of the army a terrified man ready to sign his life away for a $5,000 salary.

While Mr. Schwartz meant well, I didn't love the idea of someone else determining my worth. I soon became detached from the notion of working hard for someone else, and from Mr. Schwartz's well-meant gesture came the realization that I wanted to be the one who was in control of what I earned and how I lived. You would think that as a young veteran, husband, and new father, I would be grateful for the spoils this job offered, but I couldn't shake the ever-present thought that this was not my destiny. I was good at what I did and wanted to take my career completely into my own hands. These thoughts were the seeds of my entrepreneurial desire, and I began to consider my options.

I was nervous, to say the least, about walking away from the stability Squirt Togs provided my family and me, but I knew I needed to explore the concept of creating something for myself. Thankfully, Joan trusted my judgment and there was never a conflict at home over the enormous risk I was about to take. Soon after this epiphany, I approached my pal Nat Peters—a red-headed Holocaust survivor who managed Squirt Togs' operations and production line. After a bit of convincing, we each scraped up $12,000 via savings and a few friendly loans and took off to start our own business.

Childrenswear manufacturing was what we knew, and sales was my strength. Nat and I began setting up our new business and planning for the future. Paperwork for establishing a corporation required us to submit three potential names for the business to be vetted and approved. I wanted an appropriate name for an apparel line like Harvard or Edgewater, but everything I landed on seemed to be taken. I was stuck on a third option until one night when I was on the phone with my lawyer, and *Dobie Gillis* was on television in the background. "Dobie! Submit that," I told Nat. Although neither of us thought we would end up using that name out of the three, it wound up being the one name that was accepted on our application.

On May 3, 1960, Dobie Originals opened its doors, and our tagline at the time was *"No, no, no! Not Dopey ... DOBIE Originals!"* This is how we announced the opening of our business. One of the manufacturing contractors Nat and I knew had generously offered us a small space in his loft office near NYU. We had a little desk in the dressing room of the factory, and when the women took their breaks, we would have to leave. Everything was real now, and I was as terrified as I was determined and trusting in my abilities.

Relying on my skills as a merchant, I selected fabrics and garment designs I thought would work for the market. We cut all the fabric, paid the contractor to sew the garments, and began to develop our product line. I had no clue how it would all turn out, but I was willing to give it a try.

As word spread that I had left Squirt Togs—which had been renamed Knitmates—my former company's management spread a rumor that I had stolen some of the samples to start my own line. I knew I hadn't stolen from anyone and had relied on the knowledge I had gained, as well as my instincts, to build a completely original brand. It rapidly became apparent that my product looked nothing like anything Knitmates carried, and buyers laughed off the rumors while placing orders with me.

The growth of our company relied on bank loans, which, in those days, were obtained via the rapport one had with the banker as opposed to the rigorous credit system of today. I had a good relationship with my banker, and I was able to explain my plans and justifications in such a way that he felt confident lending me the money. Being a brand-new business, I paid every bill on time in order to ensure my access to the bank's money whenever I needed it. In the '60s, honesty and integrity were the factors that determined loan candidacy, unlike the bureaucratic model of today.

I was always looking for new ways to expand our product line. At the time, *Davy Crockett* was a wildly popular mainstream Western movie that the American masses could not get enough of. It felt like the whole world was singing that notorious theme song in unison: "*Davyyyy, Davy Crockett! King of the wild frontier!*"

I wondered what would happen if we took the image of Davy Crockett and slapped it on a few baby creepers. I made a few calls and acquired the rights to the image, and the Davy Crockett creepers turned out to be a hit! This was my first foray into the world of licensing, which would play a great role in my ultimate success in this industry.

We did a million dollars in our first year, and Nat and I went over to the west side of Manhattan where the dealerships were, and bought matching Cadillacs. *This will never happen again*, I thought, *so why not live large while we had the chance!*

We outgrew our makeshift dressing room office and moved the operation into a loft at 721 Broadway, where many contractors did their business. Dobie Originals was gaining respect, and retailers appreciated how we ran our business, which allowed us to grow enough to take a second floor in the loft. Orders were flying in. I always maintained a well-kept warehouse and exceptional working conditions for our production staff, as memories of the deplorable conditions at the factory in which my mother worked remained present in my mind.

By day, I stayed focused on building my business, expanding the line with new ideas, and reaping the rewards of a perpetually growing roster of clients. At home, I enjoyed the typical life of a young suburban family. It was a good time in my life, and my family and I were comfortable. I had arrived. I was happy. And I was living life without any clue of the devastation that was heading my way.

Me enjoying the dad life, teaching my sons how to use a bow and arrow.

Chapter 5

My Joan

By THE TIME I TURNED TWENTY-EIGHT, I HAD ACCOMplished more than I could have ever imagined. I was married to Joan, who was a wonderful wife and mother to our two healthy sons. Together, we enjoyed the typical life of a young, suburban Long Island family, and were even able to join a beach club on the South Shore. It was 1961 and my business was solidifying and continuing to grow. As hard as I was working, I can't remember ever being happier than I was during those moments. During my teenage years following my father's death, I never thought any of this would be possible.

One afternoon, Joan casually mentioned an ache in her left breast. While it wasn't severe pain, she felt an undeniable discomfort and knew something was wrong. We went to a local ob-gyn who came highly recommended, and were both relieved to hear that the diagnosis was cystic mastitis, a benign breast disease common to many women, which typically worsens during that time of the month. The doctor told us that the disease—while tedious and uncomfortable—was rather manageable and relatively harmless, and Joan was prescribed a light pain medication for her comfort. We left the doctor's office and returned to our regular lives with the understanding that we now had a minor and manageable issue to take care of.

Joan and me on our wedding day (photo to the left)
and us at a function, enjoying married life (photo to the right).

Joan continued to complain, and as much as I believed that she was simply irritated by the discomfort that the doctor warned us about, we agreed that it would be smart to get a second opinion. Relief washed over both of us once again as the second doctor diagnosed her with the same type of benign cystic mastitis with full confidence. It wasn't an ideal situation, but we both took solace in the fact that it was a tedious condition rather than a fatal disease.

I then began to notice a slight personality change in her. Joan was always the lighthearted one, full of life and energy, but the discomfort was taking an obvious toll and her light seemed to dim. Moments of irritability started to become more frequent, but I chalked it up to her inability to cope with the discomfort. To this day, my biggest regret remains the fact that I became visibly annoyed with her sporadic complaining and newfound irritability. I tried to convince her that she was okay and that she'd just need to be strong and continue to fight through it, since we had two major physicians describe the same condition. She held her head up, doing everything she could to keep it together and exude the kind and loving personality for which she was known and revered.

Joan continued to take her medication, but it was clear that she wasn't getting better or even able to maintain a status quo. She seemed to be getting worse, but stayed calm and managed to quell her complaining and irritability despite her ever-growing discomfort.

One Sunday afternoon, my family and I were visiting my sister Rita and her family in Great Neck, and Joan confided in Rita about the fact that her discomfort seemed to be getting worse, as opposed to subsiding. Rita was shocked when Joan revealed the condition of her breast, and she wasted no time arranging an appointment with her doctor in the city. This would be the first female doctor Joan would see about her condition, and Rita was adamant that this follow-up was the only way forward. This time, Joan did not receive the same diagnosis. Rita's doctor knew that Joan was suffering from something much worse than cystic mastitis, and immediately referred her to Sloan Kettering to see Dr. Norman Treves—one of the country's top breast specialists—for further analysis.

Shortly after Joan's visit I received an urgent call from Dr. Treves, asking me to come see him. I arrived at his office alone and he sat me down, unable to mask the look of concern on his face. After a pause that seemed like forever, he cleared his throat and in a near whisper, he quietly explained what Joan was facing:

"Mr. Lane, we have a problem," Dr. Treves said from behind his desk. "Your wife has a terminal illness that has unfortunately spread too far. There is nothing we can do for her."

I felt like I'd gotten hit by a bus. I nearly fainted and then went into a state of shock, doing my best to muster up the words I needed to ask about the time frame of it all.

"What does all of this mean?" I asked him, desperate for some sort of comforting fact or upside to this scenario.

It wasn't easy for Dr. Treves to walk me through the details, but he did his best to calmly inform me that in spite of Joan being so young and seemingly healthy, the illness was beginning to take over her body. In a soft and saddened tone, he finished by saying that he expected Joan to only survive with this disease for a year—eighteen months if we were lucky. I was overwhelmed with emotions I couldn't name, drowning in my own shock and disbelief. My natural denial led me to bring Joan to several other doctors for more testing—all of whom confirmed the terminal diagnosis.

Cancer. In those days, it was a swear word. A taboo utterance no one ever dared speak and a problem that seemed light-years away from any of our lives. Or so we thought. Needless to say, I crumbled.

I was in shock and utter disbelief, without any idea of where to go next. I returned to my office. Shattered. The life I shared with Joan and our two boys was everything I had ever wanted, but now I felt as if the ground were no longer beneath my feet. I shared my devastation with my business partner Nat, and his response secured him a place in my heart for the rest of my days:

"Paul, take whatever you need. Whatever money we have in the company, take it. Help her."

I was unwilling to accept the futility of the situation and continued to insist to myself and those around me that I was going to beat this thing no matter what it took. The doctors and I acknowledged the fact that we were facing a severe situation, but even in those conversations, the word *cancer* was never uttered. I decided I would spare Joan the awful truth about her diagnosis, and I continued to reiterate that she would be okay and we would get through this. Today, this decision would not have been acceptable, but at the time I believed that she would suffer less if she didn't know what was really happening. Only a handful of my closest confidantes knew. And telling my sons? Forget it. It was absolutely impossible for me to wrap my brain around the words I would need to tell them that their mother was dying. I held it all in and fought the fight, hoping for the best.

I did my research and found Dr. Cranston Holman—a breast surgeon at New York Hospital. I never took Joan back to Sloan Kettering because I never wanted her to hear the word *cancer*, so I convinced the doctors from Sloan Kettering to perform Joan's treatments at New York Hospital. Dr. Holman felt that removing her breast was the most productive way forward. Joan agreed to the surgery, and in no time, she went in for her mastectomy. It wasn't until Dr. Holman had Joan on the operating table with surgery well underway that he realized that the problem was much worse than they had originally diagnosed. The cancer had continued to spread farther throughout her body; it had infested her ovaries and lymph nodes. He stopped everything and rushed out into the waiting room to share the news with me. As my heart broke all over again, he continued to insist that we proceed with the surgery and remove Joan's breast as planned. This way, she would wake up, see her breast was gone, and assume the surgery was a success. Dr. Holman was compassionate in this suggestion, urging me that at this point, the best thing we could do for her was provide peace of mind.

I was far outside of my league here, and in a space that I found impossible to even comprehend, let alone navigate. This was a huge decision for any kid to make in his twenties, but all I heard was that this would be the best thing for Joan's well-being, and at that point, I cared about nothing else. With a shattered heart, I gave Dr. Holman the okay to proceed with Joan's mastectomy.

To this day, I have never been sure if I made the right decision, but my priority was truly Joan, her comfort, and ultimately her mental health—and at the time I thought it was a viable plan. It was for her psychological benefit, and I planned to put on whatever act was necessary to aid in her mental stability and comfort.

Hours later, Joan woke up from surgery with her left breast removed and the assumption that the doctors had completed what they needed to do in order for her to get better. But she was beside herself with horror over the physical condition in which the surgery had left her.

"How are you ever going to look at me?!" Joan cried to me during her treacherous and physically draining recovery. Mastectomies in the '60s aren't like they are today. The scarring and the stitches were horrific, and Joan was overcome with the worry that I would never look at her the same.

"It doesn't matter; you're beautiful no matter what," I constantly reassured her, but the truth was the surgery was nowhere near delicate, and it had left an incredibly gruesome scar. We bought wraps and special shirts for her to attempt to cover it so we could do our best to live as outwardly normal a life as possible. She was physically strong and never complained after this surgery, but her body was infested with cancer and I refused to share this secret, my insurmountable fear, and ultimate uncertainty of what the future held for her.

I continued to do my best to maintain a sense of normalcy in our home. Our family life changed dramatically, and the focus was solely on Joan's care. Joan did her best to be the mother our sons needed, but they inevitably took a backseat to the illness. It was clear that she needed help, so I hired Edna—your typical nanny— who was jovial, resourceful, and able to fill in the gaps when it came to what the boys needed. After all, I was still in the midst of building a business, and Joan was too weak to be everything the boys needed. Edna was truly lovely and managed to care for Joan and the boys in such a way that a great deal of weight was lifted off my shoulders. It was a small consolation amidst a horrific setting, in which I was perpetually devastated, scared, and struggling with my decision to shelter Joan from the morbid truth of her condition.

Desperate for a distraction for all of us, I went looking for a bigger and better house to purchase. I thought that buying a new home would offer diversion from the focus on Joan's illness, and give everyone something to look forward to. I found a wonderful home in Roslyn, Long Island, twice the size of our house at the time in a beautifully quaint neighborhood. Joan was excited and was looking eagerly at her seemingly bright future.

The new house lifted her spirits, and she became very involved in domestic life. She decorated with such excitement, and took such great care of our boys. We would still go out to dinner and continue with our social calendar. My business was flourishing, and for a handful of fleeting moments, our future seemed bright again. Here she was, excited as could be about her new home and without the slightest hint of the severity of her condition. While she was strong, she was still in pain and discomfort, and curiosity eventually led her to inquire about the truth.

"Paul, am I dying?" she asked me one night as she lay next to me in bed.

"No, honey, you're not," I reassured her. "We have a problem. It's complicated, but we have to keep going forward."

"Are you sure?"

"Yes," I replied, knowing full well the truth would do more harm than good. My chosen approach seemed so necessary at the time, and I felt like this façade was maintaining her mental well-being and ultimately saving her life.

Two months later, I connected with Dr. Artie Pazanos—a world-renowned endocrinologist who took a fast and strong liking to Joan, as everyone seemed to do. Dr. Pazanos became a pillar in our lives and eventually a dear friend, and she never gave up hope that we would find a solution to Joan's perpetually worsening condition. She introduced us to a renowned brain surgeon who was quickly gaining recognition in his field for his cutting-edge, life-saving procedures. He posed the idea of lifting Joan's brain to remove her pituitary gland and replacing any lost hormones with prescription drugs. This would quell the aggressive spreading of the cancer and could potentially add years to her life. We explained this option to Joan, and in spite of the fact that she still had yet to hear the C-word for herself, she bravely agreed. I was overwhelmed at the magnitude of the procedure, but at that point was willing to try anything. Joan's toughness and bravery were astounding following this surgery, and she never once complained about her pain, maintaining her typical demeanor of kindness, innocence, and love.

It was November 22, 1963, and Joan was still in the hospital recovering. Doctors came to me that morning with news that the surgery appeared to have been successful, and to their measure it would seem as if the cancer had stopped spreading. The despair that had become a mainstay in my life was washed away by the euphoria this news brought. *Finally,* I thought, *we're going to win!*

There was a spring in my step that morning as I walked over to the subway on the east side of the city to get back to my office and start another workday. I walked down the stairs into the subway, paid my fare, and waited on the platform for the next train to bring me downtown.

Suddenly, screams echoed across the subway platform, and strangers began embracing each other while crying frantically.

"President Kennedy was shot in Dallas!" one woman screamed, and in an instant, the relief I felt from Joan's positive prognosis was quickly replaced by a wave of sadness. It's astounding how drastically your reality can change in a moment.

In the coming days, the nation was at a standstill, gripped with fear and locked in mourning for our assassinated president. As the country faced the fallout of President Kennedy's untimely and shocking death, President Johnson took over as commander in chief, and the nation braced itself for a future that was uncertain at best.

But amidst the national mayhem, there was hope in our home, and life seemed like it was finally starting to return to normal. Joan was released from the hospital with medication that would replace the hormones lost during the removal of her pituitary gland, and it appeared that she was on her way to recovery. For a brief moment in time, a feeling of lightness returned to our home. Joan's bandages were removed, and a wig would cover the scars on her head. The smile never seemed to fade from her face, and her persona seemed to be returning, much to the delight of everyone around her.

We carried on with our lives, with Joan relying on an artillery of medication and frequent hospital visits to monitor her progress and recovery. Unfortunately, Joan's progress halted, and the doctors informed me that the illness had reverted to its worsened state. There I was, once again, faced with the decision to shelter Joan from the truth—which I did, with the same well-intentioned hopes I'd held onto since the beginning of this tragic scenario.

The weight of the truth of Joan's condition started to take a toll on me, and I began to drink in an attempt to detach from my reality as best I could. It started to become the only thing that soothed me, but friends took notice and quickly intervened.

"You have a big job to do, Paul," remarked my good friend Nat Bernard. "You need to stay sharp." Nat took me to Dr. Frank Berchenko, an analytic psychiatrist who once worked alongside Sigmund Freud. He took me on as a crisis patient and offered strategies for dealing with the impossible situation I was facing in a more intelligent manner. Under Dr. Berchenko's guidance I quickly became able to cope and navigate more effectively, and I continued to stay focused.

It was now the summer of 1964, and Joan's condition was on a steady decline. But as weak as she was—sometimes to the point of being bedridden—she still never complained. Not once. She handled it all with such grace and dignity, and we continued to do our best to lead a normal life. Our boys were off at summer camp, and I was able to drive out to see them on visiting day. When I saw them enjoying their summer without a care in the world, guilt and despair washed over me with the realization that their mother might not live long enough for them to ever see her again. Thankfully, when they returned home from camp at the end of August, she was still alive. She did as much as she could to be present for them, but they continued to be swept aside, and caring for her remained the priority in our household.

The outpouring of support from our friends and family was overwhelming—a true testament to how loved Joan was by everyone she encountered.

Not a day went by when we didn't have friends and family in our home who had come to show love to Joan and offer support to the boys and me. I remember my sister Rita and her husband were about to head off to Paris, and came to visit one last time before they embarked on the trip they had been planning for months. Joan mentioned how much she would miss Rita, and how much she had come to rely on her. I mentioned this to Rita and her husband, and in the blink of an eye their bags were unpacked and my brother-in-law was on the phone with the airline, cancelling their tickets. Rita was back at Joan's bedside that same evening without a second thought. This is just another wonderful example of how loved Joan was and how extraordinarily caring my sister Rita always seemed to be.

As her condition continued to worsen, our physician at the time, Dr. Bob Bailiff, urged me to bring her to the hospital, and I did. She stayed there for a couple of days, and the doctors were out of options.

"We can't let her live like this anymore, Paul," Dr. Bailiff pleaded with me over the phone. "Let her go. It's time."

I couldn't do it. Even though I had been preparing myself for this moment for over two years, I wasn't ready. But I knew that she was in more pain than any human could bear. I agreed to let Dr. Bailiff move her into hospice in order to provide as much comfort for her as possible in her final moments.

On September 13, 1964, the phone rang at two in the morning, and my heart sank immediately. That night was a blur, and my only clear memories are of hearing the words, "She's gone," through the phone, and then being with her at her bedside seemingly moments later. As she lay there still and peaceful, I spoke calmly to her and did my best to say my goodbyes for what to this day remain the worst hours of my life. Some time passed, and I picked myself up and drove home to take on a task I had feared the most since the day I'd been given her diagnosis.

I arrived home to find our two boys sitting on the stairs: nine-year-old Jeffrey on the lower step and seven-year-old Curtis a few steps higher. They knew something was up, and they were waiting for me to get home with an update.

"Your mother is gone," I managed to choke out. It took all my might. Curtis fell apart sobbing while Jeffrey simply froze. The three of us sat there for what seemed like an eternity, overwhelmed with devastation. While I ultimately knew this day was inevitable, I was absolutely unprepared for the moment it finally happened. Nothing would have allowed me to avoid my heart shattering into a million pieces at the moment of loss, and the time between that moment and her funeral was a whirlwind of despair.

Joan with sons. Joan with our sons, Curtis (right)
and Jeffrey (left) before she passed.

I did the best that I could to arrange her service, which was held at Riverside Memorial. As people waited for the procession to begin, I refused to let anyone move her coffin out of the small holding room. I still couldn't let her go. At every phase of this devastating ordeal, I wasn't able to let her go.

"Get the fuck away!" I screamed as people banged on the door, insisting I let them in and let the casket out. It was all so surreal.

When I finally let go and allowed the service to proceed, I was blown away by the sheer magnitude of attendance. Riverside Memorial is no small venue, yet they ran out of seats, and attendees spilled out into the lobby and onto the front steps. I had never seen anything like this before, and the impact my wonderful Joan had had on so many lives became crystal clear.

The next few months were spent on autopilot. I grew to resent my suburban neighborhood because of the happy families that surrounded me, and I could no longer exist in a house full of memories that Joan and I had shared. That Thanksgiving, the boys and I arrived at Rita's country club in Great Neck to have dinner and do our best to find some level of normalcy and family life. Seemingly happy families sat around the table, passing food and enjoying a normal existence. I sat there frozen, paralyzed with sorrow and feeling like I was missing both my arms. The grief became too much to bear, and I leaned over to Rita to ask if I could leave.

"Go ahead," she replied with understanding, and I collected my boys and got out of there. I dropped them off at the house for Edna to put them to bed, and I headed into the city and drank myself to oblivion. I never made a habit of this behavior, but that night I desperately needed a break from my cold reality.

Soon after, I put the house up for sale and was anxious to get far away from the suburban family lifestyle I had grown to love—but no longer felt I had without Joan by my side.

Edna remained with us in our house after Joan had died, and I urged her to do what she needed to in order to have her own life. She had been such a powerful force in Joan's care, and I showed my appreciation as best I could, teaching her how to drive and extending an invite to her friends and family to join her in the home for visits and meals. Perhaps it was this newfound comfort or Joan's ultimate absence, but Edna became a little too comfortable, and I started to become concerned about her presence. Things came to a halt when she decided to use her hands to discipline my son, and I fired her on the spot.

The house sold in no time, and I moved with the boys to a duplex I had rented on East 72nd Street in Manhattan—a far cry from Roslyn's suburban family life. Without Edna, I was truly a single father, scrambling to do my best in spite of my complete lack of mothering abilities.

In the blink of an eye, I was far away from the home life I knew, without Joan by my side. I was once again starting my life over, this time as a single father without a clue of what was in store or if I would even have the courage to go on. But now, I was all these two young boys had and I knew I had no choice but to navigate our way to any possible version of normalcy.

It was just the three of us, and the future had never been so unclear.

Chapter 6

Navigating Fatherhood

It was the summer of 1964. Joan was gone, and although the house was filled with wonderful memories, it felt cold and empty, and the boys and I had just moved into the apartment I rented on East 72nd Street at Park Avenue. I never really got over the loss of my wife; that type of sadness is not something you become used to. Even as I write this nearly six decades after her death, her presence and the memories we shared together are still strong, and there is a hole in my heart that could only be filled by her. Every holiday, birthday, graduation, and wedding has been flanked by my ever-present sadness over Joan not being there to bear witness to the milestones in our sons' lives.

I thought Manhattan would provide the boys and me with some version of a fresh start. I was brand new in my role as a single parent, and will forever have an unwavering respect for any man or woman who has been thrust into that role. Every day, all over the world, individuals take on the impossible task of being the sole provider and lone caregiver to children, and unless you've lived it, you can't imagine the weight of this monumental task. There are no classes or manuals for figuring out how to get through it, only folks doing their best, often amidst devastating chaos. Thankfully, I was lucky enough to have a strong support system composed of friends and family who had rallied around me in the wake of Joan's passing. The boys and I were always invited to dinners, events, and even ski trips with friends of mine, and on most Sundays, we would make the trek to Great Neck for dinner with my sister Rita, her husband Marty, and their three sons. My new life was nowhere near a quick and painless transition, nor was it seamless, but I have no idea where I would be today without the outpouring of love and support I received when I needed it the most.

Summer was well underway, and as we went through the motions of settling in to our new place, my focus became solely on getting the boys enrolled in a good school, and ideally keeping them together. Given everything they had just gone through, it was important for them to attend the same school so they could support each other, and move toward some semblance of normal adolescent life.

I visited several schools in the area and finally found Columbia Grammar School—a private school on the city's West Side. One of the administrators was sympathetic to our story, and invited me to enroll Jeffrey into the sixth grade and Curtis in the third grade for the upcoming school year. Perhaps this was because I took her on a few dates, but I can't say for sure. It was a small victory for us amidst a flurry of disappointments, and I am forever grateful to Columbia Grammar School for accepting my sons and giving me the slightest hope that we would be okay.

*My two sons, Jeffrey to the right and Curtis
on the left, all dressed up. This was at Curtis'
Bar Mitzvah.*

Throughout all of this I still had a business to run, and desperately needed a housekeeper who could keep the apartment together and the boys fed. After a few trials, I found Gerta—the quintessential German housekeeper with a keen eye for detail and commitment to cleanliness, and I tiptoed around her, careful as could be to keep everything in its place. My home was as well kept as an art gallery, and removing one pair of socks from their perfectly arranged row seemed like it could throw the entire house into disarray. But it was a comfort to know that if someone needed an emergency appendectomy, you could do it on my kitchen table, as my house always remained as clean as a hospital.

The boys were well taken care of, and it finally felt like we were all adapting as well as we could to our brand-new life. I was doing my best to adjust to the life of a single dad, but became rather self-conscious about the dark cloud that seemed to loom over my head whenever I entered a room, as smiles and laughter would be replaced by concerned eyes and the standard "Oh Paul, how are you and the kids holding up?" I grew an interest in meeting new friends.

Soon after I decided to take a stab at a social life in the city, I was introduced to a social club called The SWORDs, which stood for "Single, Widowed, or Divorced." It was an organization of single men who were relatively successful, single, and interested in socializing. The organization arranged for golf and other athletic outings, and they put on lavish parties at some of the best venues in the city, where women were invited to attend for free. I was reluctantly intrigued by the idea of networking and meeting people who were suddenly single and could relate to my experience.

I remember, at one particular event, I noticed an altercation brewing at the doorway to the restaurant where invited guests were arriving. I always considered myself a peacemaker of sorts, so I approached the men and suggested that it might be inappropriate to be carrying on this way at such an event. The next sound I heard was a set of knuckles hitting my jaw, as one of the men who didn't seem to share this opinion knocked me unconscious in one swift punch. Having never been much of a fighter growing up, I wasn't prepared for this reaction, and my six-foot-two frame folded like an accordion as I hit the pavement. It was the first and only time I have ever been knocked out. When I came to, I was told that the person who slugged me was a known gangster who felt entitled to attend the party, and I had helped stop him from making it inside. I brushed off my shoulders and walked back into the party as a makeshift hero to all the guests who'd witnessed what I had done.

The SWORDs scene quickly became something I lost interest in. What was promoted as a support group was really just a bunch of crabs in a bucket, reveling in each other's misery. Sounds of booing and hissing filled the air whenever it was announced that someone from the group had gotten engaged, but when a divorce was on the horizon, the group would cheer and celebrate a couple's ultimate failure. It was a negative environment I no longer had interest in being a part of, so I backed out of my membership.

In my continued quest to become integrated into the new neighborhood and, ultimately, my new life I joined the 92nd Street Y, where I enjoyed playing racquetball and meeting new people. Speaking of making friends, on one afternoon I was playing racquetball against someone I was randomly paired with. I swung hard at the ball and accidentally smacked it right into the center of my opponent's head, causing a deep cut and quite the scene. I went with him to the Mount Sinai Hospital, where he received stitches for the number I did on him, and then back to my place for an apology cocktail or two. We became instant friends, but shortly after the racquetball incident, he relocated to Hollywood for a production job at CBS. For a long time, we called each other to catch up, and he always remarked that he thought of me each time he combed his hair and saw the scar.

New York City has always been a great place to meet women. Friends would take me to the Gaslight—a club that emulated the classic speakeasies from the Prohibition era. While I was there, some of the women took a liking to me after hearing my story, and I wound up spending time with some of them. My routine grew very strange; I would work all day, come home to have dinner with my sons, hit the town for a few hours, and return home before my sons woke up. All the girls I met during this time in my life adored my sons, and loved when I brought them skating, skiing, or just to hang out.

My dance card filled up rather quickly, and between family, work, and fun, time was wearing thin. It wasn't easy balancing single parenthood, running a business, and having some semblance of a social life. I grew tired of spending endless hours on dinner dates with no spark, and I often found myself concocting fabricated emergencies in order to escape my date and get home. I knew this wasn't the ideal way to treat someone, so my offer to well-intentioned friends who insisted on setting me up was that I was available for coffee only—a fifteen-minute encounter in which I would determine if there was enough of a connection to warrant a dinner reservation. I would recommend this tactic today to any single person, navigating the expensive and time-consuming world of dating, which has been hyper-fueled by online dating and social media.

One of my best friends, Gene Baranoff, was a major supplier of home goods to the big retailers throughout the city, and knew plenty of important and impressive people. One day, he mentioned that he had spoken about me to one of his buyers, who in turn raved to him about her good friend Iris. I was told she was an attractive twenty-seven-year-old fashion coordinator of home furnishings at Bloomingdales in Manhattan. The two of them came to the conclusion that Iris and I must meet, and Gene shared her number with me.

By now, my business had grown into a large manufacturing facility, which I had moved to Long Island City in New York. I hosted a production meeting for my team on Monday nights, and thought this would be a good opportunity to meet Iris on my way home, since she lived on 34th Street just on the other side of the Midtown Tunnel. I called her in the early evening to suggest we meet for a drink in an hour or so, and to my surprise, she was insulted and in disbelief that I'd had the audacity to assume she would be available to meet with me a mere hour after my first phone call. I should have considered this a warning signal, but I was still interested in meeting her. She suggested that if I wanted to take her out, I should plan a proper date with adequate notice. I planned a dinner for us that Thursday, and when we finally met, I found her to be lovely, nice-looking, and connected to an arts-and-culture scene I had yet to be exposed to.

Before Iris came along, I met many lovely women through friends, family, and my business. I was flattered by the attention, but as the old expression goes: "When you're ready, you're ready," and I began to desire stability over the life of a Manhattan bachelor. Iris and I began seeing each other regularly. She cared a great deal about me and exposed me to so much life I had never before encountered—the opera, the ballet, and galleries up and down Manhattan. I always felt like a wide-eyed Brooklyn kid without much culture, enamored with the level of sophistication she brought to the table. Iris also showed an interest in the boys, and after spending time with them, she appeared to care for them as much as she did for me. I began to see potential in her, and was encouraged by my mother, sister, and close friends to pursue a more serious relationship—if for no other reason than to provide a life for my boys that resembled something close to a family. I never once considered this an act of replacing Joan, but I did long for a sense of stability. Even at my height of singlehood, I remember always being more attracted to the idea of a family than to running around the city as a bachelor. I was really not meant for the single life, and much preferred the warm and familiar feeling of having a family.

Looking back, the seeds of trouble were always there, and signs that I was making a mistake now seem glaring in hindsight. I remember meeting Iris's family for the first time at a bowling alley in White Plains. We had pizza, and when the bill came, I was made to pay for my slices. This was a red flag I should have considered, but I was caught up in the hope of a new relationship and handed over my pizza money without thinking twice. Perhaps I was too impressed by Iris, or perhaps I ignored the warning signs because I so wanted to return to family life. And in the beginning, Iris did her best to accommodate my sons and perpetuate a stable domestic life. The boys responded well and seemed to accept her in our home. So I took the natural next step and asked Iris to be my wife, after receiving so much pressure from my sister and family.

Not long after, we were married at the Fifth Avenue Synagogue, on May 20, 1966. It was a small ceremony attended by immediate family only, and I remember my boys being so happy, showing up with rice and joyfully throwing it on Iris and me as we exited the temple.

A month or two later, I rented out the catering hall in a luxury residence on East 73rd Street between Madison and Fifth Avenue and invited 125 of our friends and family members to celebrate our nuptials. Joan Crawford and President Eisenhower had thrown parties there. I figured that if it was good enough for them, it would be good enough for me. I arrived at the hall on the eve of the event, only to find that it had no air conditioning. It was over ninety degrees outside that day, and my guests and I were dripping with sweat. Women were complaining, and men were removing

62

their jackets to reveal soaking-wet, sweat-stained dress shirts. The food was awful, and it quickly became clear that the night was a disaster. As the evening finally ended, I confronted the manager and insisted I shouldn't have to pay for this hot mess but I was quickly surrounded by some of the larger wait staff who suggested that it would be in my best interest to pay. I got the hint, reluctantly handed over the money, and stormed out. I walked across Madison Avenue, furious, sweaty, and not paying attention. I failed to notice the city bus that was slowly pulling into the stop, and apparently the bus driver didn't see me either. The bus collided with me, thankfully at a slow pace, but with enough force to knock me to the ground. I was now rolling around on the pavement in my brand-new suit, as the bus driver ran frantically out of the bus, barreling toward me as scared as could be. I knew I wasn't seriously hurt, and I suggested that he should leave me alone and get back on his bus, as I was simply having a really bad day. I ended up suing the caterer and recovering some of my money, but that evening wound up setting the tone for my years to come with Iris.

Life began once again, but the cost of living in Manhattan with two boys in private school and a heavy roster of extracurricular activities became burdensome. I moved my family once again to the suburbs, deciding on a home located in the neighborhood of Lake Success in Great Neck—it was close to the Manhattan line with great schools and a young family feel. We went on with our lives; Iris stopped working, and I continued to work in the city. My two boys once again started at a new school, and they were as easygoing with it all as I could have hoped. Even though the loss was huge for them, they were able to adjust almost seamlessly, and never gave much trouble.

Their mother was not as present in their minds as she was in mine, which allowed them to be open to Iris, and they gravitated toward a home life reminiscent of an actual family. Curtis was a great student who worked hard, and an athlete who excelled in swimming and tennis. Jeffrey was less into athletics and leaned more toward music and girls. Iris did try her best, but lacked that warm, mothering aspect.

Hints of problems continued to surface, and Iris's jealousy was ever present, but I did my best to ignore and overlook it. I was loyal to a fault, but if a woman even spoke to me, Iris would have a fit. I had a collection of letters from Joan that I had kept from the time we wrote to each other when I was in the service, typical letters between two young lovebirds during wartime, addressing our love for each other and fears for the future. They were nothing more than sweet musings about how she spent her days and how much she missed me, but during this time we got to know each other letter by letter, and they became something I cherished. I kept them in a small box in my storage room and would read them from time to time. I never viewed this as a betrayal of Iris, but rather a collection of memories I liked to revisit from time to time with the intention of keeping Joan's memory alive. Iris didn't share my opinion, and felt it was inappropriate for me to keep these letters. One day, I entered our storage room to find that Iris had taken it upon herself to destroy and discard every last letter and the envelopes that held them. The only tangible reminders of conversations between Joan and me were lost forever, and I was devastated and furious.

I was seething with rage. *How could she be so selfish?!* I thought as I got my lawyers on the phone to inquire about a divorce. Unless you've experienced losing the love of your life at such a young age, you will never understand the grip that person will have on your heart for eternity. My marriage with Iris had already been unraveling, not to mention how difficult it was to be married to someone who didn't accept that there was a life before her, especially since Iris had quite the sordid past as a single woman. Let's just say I often wondered how she made it up the ladder in retail. I wanted out of this marriage as quickly as divorce papers could be drawn up; however, my lawyer didn't see this as the best way forward. He urged me to stay—if for nothing else than to continue to give the boys the structure and stability of a family life. He successfully convinced me not to start divorce proceedings, but I would never forgive nor forget Iris's decision to destroy something so precious because of misguided jealousy.

From that moment on, our home was functional but not warm. I threw all my energy into my business and maintaining a peaceful home life. As the years went by, Iris began pressuring me into having another child, and I reluctantly agreed. To this point, we were a family of boys; I had two sons and my sister had three, so it was assumed that another son was on the way. But on October 4, 1968, my beautiful daughter Tracey was born. I was ecstatic and immediately fell head over heels in love with her.

I brought Tracey home, but Iris had to stay in the hospital to take care of gall bladder issues. I hired a baby nurse who came well-recommended to take care of Tracey while I was at work. One afternoon, the boys were at school and I was in a meeting when I received a frantic call from the nurse. She wasn't making sense and sounded either drunk or delusional as she slurred through confusing sentences that seemed to allude to my daughter being either hurt or in danger. I called the police and urged them to kick down my door as I waited for a car to take me home. Thankfully, the police found my daughter safe and sound and removed the nurse, who had either suffered from a psychotic break or had taken something and lost control. I was so grateful Tracey was okay, and the fallout from this ordeal motivated me to help Iris have even just a few moments with her. During one of my visits with Iris at the hospital, I draped a coat over her, snuck her out the back door, and drove her home to see Tracey. The doctors weren't too pleased with me, but I felt it was worth it. Who knows what could have happened if I'd never received that frantic phone call.

This was my introduction to Tracey. Relationships between fathers and sons are intrinsically different than those between fathers and daughters. We were attached at the hip and I took her everywhere, and from the moment I met her up until this very day, Tracey has remained my pride and joy. There is a great deal of truth to the old saying, "A son is a son till he gets a wife, but a daughter is a daughter all her life."

My business continued to grow, and I was enjoying the suburban family life as much as I could. I started playing golf at the local club on Lake Success, and wound up making it to the club championships. I ended up losing on the eighteenth hole to a dentist I wasn't fond of, who couldn't seem to stop himself from flirting with my wife at every opportunity. I was annoyed and decided that I didn't need any more stress in my private life. Work was stressful and maintaining peace in my home had been stressful, so why continue with golf if it was nothing more than extra stress? So I threw out my golf clubs and sought an activity that would provide the relaxation I needed from the extracurricular activities

I was a part of. This led me to discover a passion for boating, which became a major part of my life for nearly four decades to come.

I felt like our family was overdue for a vacation, so I booked all five of us as, well as our nanny, into a villa for a month in the South of France. The beach, sightseeing, and accommodations were spectacular, and everyone looked to be enjoying themselves. Except for Iris, who seemed to be perpetually obsessed with what others had and didn't have, while showing no gratitude for the life I was providing for her. Friends of ours from Long Island had traveled to a villa nearby, and when Iris heard the husband had bought his wife a collection of scarfs, she immediately felt shortchanged and called me out for not doing the same. I was furious—here we were in this elaborate villa for a month, and Iris was upset because she didn't receive a scarf. It was the first and only time I ever slapped her—or any woman for that matter. Not my proudest moment, but she wore me down to the point of unfathomable frustration, and I reacted poorly.

I eventually moved the family back to the city and into an apartment on Park Avenue. While my kids were happy and healthy, my marriage never seemed to get better. I considered Iris's and my relationship like the ocean. The surface appeared serene and calm, but underneath was an undertow of unpleasantness—completely unstable and constantly pulling me down. It was thirteen years of one incident after another, and neither of us was anything that even resembled happy.

I was able to enroll Tracey in the Lenox School in Manhattan. Jeffrey got into George Washington University. And Curtis got into the Wharton School of Business. As Curtis got older, he grew noticeably less fond of Iris. Perhaps this was leftover hostility from

Iris taking almost no photos of Curtis during family functions—a pattern that became especially noticeable to him after there were so few pictures taken of him at his own bar mitzvah, as if he weren't even there. But I knew Curtis had picked up on something similar to what I had noticed, and he developed an unwavering dislike for his stepmother. Jeffrey was a much different story, and he will attest to feeling a connection to Iris and actually having a bond with her. He attributes this to the fact that I carried high hopes for my boys and had a tendency to be a tough man with strict expectations. Iris would often defend Jeffrey in menial disputes about little things, and in her he found an ally in our home. Much later in life, Jeffrey began to notice aspects of Iris's character that he didn't appreciate, and he has since cut ties, but unlike his brother, he was quite fond of her growing up.

Incidents of mayhem continued to surround Tracey. I still get goose bumps when I think about the night I was awakened by the phone. It was an odd hour for someone to call me at home, so I figured something must be wrong.

"Mr. Lane, I know where you live and where your daughter goes to school," said the muffled, heavily accented voice on the other end of the phone.

"What?!" Who is this?" I demanded, slowly coming to my senses and realizing that there was sheer evil on the other end of this call.

"I'm not asking for much, but I need you to give me $10,000 in cash or else I'm taking your daughter," the voice on the other end continued. "I need to get out of the country immediately!"

"What?!" I shrieked, overcome as terror rushed through my veins. Whoever was on the other end of the phone instructed me to leave a bag containing $10,000 in a specific dumpster in Long

Island City in order to avoid Tracey being kidnapped. I dropped the phone and rushed into Tracey's bedroom to make sure she was still there. Once I saw her sleeping soundly without a clue of the mayhem that was currently spiraling around her, I called the FBI. They wished me well, but said that since Tracey hadn't been kidnapped yet, there was nothing they could do. "Call us back after she gets kidnapped," were their parting instructions. I initially thought that it was someone playing an evil prank on me. However, as the phone calls became frequent and the threats became heightened, it was clear that the person on the other end of the line knew my daughter, Tracey, and me, and it was terrifyingly evident that this was a serious issue that could not be ignored.

The NYPD were much more helpful and responsive than the FBI, and several detectives walked me through the process of fulfilling this prospective kidnapper's request and keeping Tracey out of harm's way. The plan was to appear as if I were complying with this crook's demands and complete the drop with police nearby but strategically out of plain sight. The bag I would drop would be filled with blank paper in order to appear as if it were stuffed with cash, and the eyes of the law would remain fixed on the drop-off point until the bag was collected, at which time cops would descend on the would-be kidnapper and make an arrest.

The next time the wannabe kidnapper called me with his demands, I agreed to drop the money in a dumpster he chose, located in Long Island City, Queens. With hidden police eyes watching my every step, I arrived by car at the drop-off location. I stepped out of the car, walked over to the dumpster the kidnapper had chosen, and tossed the bag inside. I then returned to the car as nonchalantly as I was able to, in spite of my heart beating in my throat. I waited for a few moments to see if anyone approached the dumpster, and much to our dismay, a garbage truck pulled up and sanitation workers lifted and emptied the dumpster into the truck with the rest of that day's trash. I guess no one thought to look at the trash collection schedule amidst the planning of this sting operation, and here we were.

I didn't know what was to come of this and waited for the kidnapper to call me again, so we could pick up where we'd left off. He finally did and proposed a new plan. At this point, I had moved Tracey to a secured location so she would remain safe and out of harm's way while I fended off this kidnapper as best I could. He finally called again to inform me of his next round of demands.

"What a terrible thing to have happen to you," the kidnapper said, condescendingly. He then offered me a break as a result of the unbelievable mishap of the garbage truck accidentally collecting the duffel bag. He only asked me for $5,000 this time, but provided more information about who I was and where I lived to instill a sense of urgency in the process. I shared this update with the detectives, but they informed me that if we caught him and sent him to prison, upon his release, he would pose an even bigger threat to my family and me. The NYPD provided me with a script of what to say to the kidnapper, who we figured out was a two-bit criminal who had once been employed as one of my drivers, occasionally dropping my daughter off at school. I followed this unconventional advice, picked up the phone, and aggressively read through the entire script, which started off with the phrase, "Listen, you motherfucker," and proceeded to make various threats that were to be honored if he didn't leave my family alone. I told him that I knew exactly who he was and that if he continued to make these threats, he would be prosecuted and spend the rest of his days rotting in a prison cell. I hung up the phone and never heard from him again, but I felt uneasy for a long period of time afterward and ensured that there were appropriate eyes on Tracey to ensure her continued safety.

This was just one of many dramatic tales from the life of my daughter, but to this day, we've somehow managed to navigate the drama and tragedy with the courage to go on.

The biggest regret I have from this time in my life is something that I believe my son Curtis will never forgive me for. He went away to Wharton Business School, and soon after he left, I converted his bedroom into a guest room, thinking that it wouldn't matter since he wasn't home often and had grown out of his teenage quarters.

Big mistake.

I truly was well intentioned, thinking that he knew he always had a place to stay, but looking back, I believe that this choice I made was the catalyst for our drifting apart. I also believe wholeheartedly that I forced a detachment that he never wanted. He was so hurt by my converting his bedroom without asking him, that he did what he needed to do to protect his heart, which was, ultimately, to pull away from me. To this day, I often wonder if I planted that seed by taking his bedroom away and unintentionally sending a message that he wasn't wanted or welcome. When he built his home, he made quite certain that there was plenty of room for his boys, even making a comment that no one would ever be able to take his boys' rooms from them. I had no idea at the time that my actions would cause this much damage, but knowing what I know now, if I had the chance to do it over, I never would have touched his room.

Unlike Curtis, who seemed to have had a linear path since

childhood and a focused goal—to rise through the ranks of big business—Jeffrey struggled with a lack of direction and was seemingly unable to pick a path. He also struggled with some of his studies, and seemed to be lost and spiraling down a dark path of dangerous life choices. He was having a difficult first year of college at George Washington University when I heard about the Lyndon School in England through a psychiatrist in D.C. whom I was fortunate enough to connect with through a doctor in New York. I thought that the open-format curriculum would help him to explore himself and figure out what he wanted from life, while yanking him out of this black hole. Jeffrey spent two years there, and I was instructed to keep communication to a minimum in order to allow him to grow and develop through learning programs that focused on self-acceptance and autonomy. I followed these instructions and left him alone, and he returned with such self-esteem and comfort in the fact that it was okay to think differently and explore any and everything he desired. I truly believe this program saved his life.

One fateful afternoon in October of 1981, I received a call from my friend Gene—the same man who had introduced Iris and me all those years back. His daughter had been institutionalized with depression and was begging him to let her come home. I'm not sure if he simply wanted to talk about it or was calling to ask my opinion, given my experience in the army as a neuropsychiatric technician tasked with the responsibility of suicide prevention, among other things, but I urged him to keep her in there, at least for a little while longer.

"This kind of healing takes time," I remarked, doing my best to explain to Gene that this was in her best interest and was not, in fact, as cruel as his daughter was claiming it all was.

He didn't take my advice, and less than an hour after her arrival home, she had jumped from their apartment window to her death. I was in a meeting at the time, as my advertising executive Brenda walked me through a pitch to acquire the license to use the name Playskool on some of our clothing. Gene's voice was a flurry of screaming and sobbing on the other end of the phone, and I cut the meeting short and rushed to his home. I accompanied him and his wife to the morgue and stood beside them as the coroner pulled the sheet back from his daughter's lifeless body so they could provide a positive identification. The sound of shrill screams I had never before heard a human make is something I would never forget, and I clutched him tight as I walked him back to the car. I returned home in a daze and sat next to the phone sat with a bottle of scotch and a glass. With each swig, I would dial Gene's friends and family one by one to break the news.

I did my best to stay as calm as I could as people on the other end of the phone were falling to pieces. Gene's only request at this time was solitude. He desperately wanted to be left alone, and I was tasked with instructing friends and family to give him space. He didn't want any extra people around, but Iris treated it all like a social affair and insisted she would go over. That day was one of the longest days of my life, as I ended up at Gene's house without Iris—at Gene's request.

I returned home after four in the morning when all was said and done, and Iris greeted me, irate with anger because she'd felt excluded from the event. *How has she managed to make this about her without any concern of what I've gone through?!* I wondered with disgust. At that moment, I was done. This was truly the last straw.

"Fuck it, I'm outta here," I thought to myself, and never looked back.

I moved into the Kitano Hotel and once again contacted my lawyers—this time to leave for good.

Iris became ruthless. She hired one of the city's toughest divorce lawyers, and I had enlisted one of Donald Trump's attorneys. Needless to say, it was a gritty process. The new law of equitable distribution was just being passed, and since I was now the CEO of a public company, my lawyer urged me to agree to give Iris a strong settlement for the sake of a clean break and minimal press. I agreed and wanted it done, but come closing day, an extra clause had been added. The addendum stated that I was to pay all expenses pertaining to Tracey, from tuition to clothing to marriage, and any other needs that might arise. I instantly saw red. For me it was a no-brainer: my kids were always taken care of and wanted for nothing, but the idea that someone was trying to legislate how I took care of my daughter via some court document like I was some sort of deadbeat had me seething with rage. I quickly explained to Iris and her attorneys that not only was I not signing a single page, but also, if they failed to remove the clause about Tracey, I would put every dollar I had in barrels and toss them in the East River, and neither Iris nor our attorneys would ever see a penny. *Try me.* They deleted the clause, and after a two-year battle, I finally signed the divorce papers in November of 1984. I was back to being a single man, utterly soured on the desire to ever marry again—or so I thought.

Chapter 7

Sheila's Return

I HAVE NEVER BEEN ONE TO GIVE UP WITHOUT A fight. Years before ending my marriage to Iris, I tried attending marriage counseling with my then-wife to seek anything that resembled a peaceful marriage. Dr. Gerald Emmet treated us. He was a Freudian-trained psychoanalyst who helped couples communicate better and essentially learn how to hate each other as little as possible.

During our ongoing treatment, Dr. Emmet called a meeting with all of his patients to share the news that he no longer believed that psychoanalysis was an effective way to treat patients, and he would be closing his practice. His plan was to move to India to pursue a new methodology of mindfulness based on Buddhist principles. A couple of years later, Dr. Emmet returned, having studied under monks, gurus, and traditionalists, and now going by the name Nirgrantha. He shared some of what he had learned and spoke highly of the wondrous effects of meditation and truly living in the moment. I was intrigued by what he was sharing with us and began delving into the world of mindfulness and the "Be here now" way of life. I began attending panels and meditations led by world-renowned authors, teachers, and spiritual leaders, and to this day, meditation and mindfulness remains important for me, and I practice them regularly.

One Friday evening, I sat in a coffee shop in New York with a small meditation group that was led by Mandara, a woman in her early fifties who worked with Negrantha and claimed to have psychic abilities. We were going around the table sharing unfulfilled parts of our lives, and I decided to open up about the secret I had kept for twenty-eight years.

I chose to share the story of the younger sister I had but never knew. I shared the details of my mother being hauled off in an ambulance. I explained that I'd assumed she was dying, since mere months earlier, my father had been hauled from our home by emergency responders in the exact same fashion, and the next time I had seen him was at his funeral. The pain from that experience was still fresh, and with great devastation, I assumed it was happening all over again. I described how I'd pretended to sleep as my Uncle Jack explained to my sister that our mom had given birth to a baby girl and immediately gave her up for adoption. I finished my story with a hopeful summation about the possibility of one day crossing paths with the sister I'd never known.

As I finished telling the story, I noticed that Mandara seemed to be overcome with anxiety, and she was shaking.

"Paul," she said abruptly, staring fiercely into my eyes as if to ensure my focus was solely on what she was about to say, "your sister is looking for you."

It felt like a scene out of a movie.

I reacted the way most people would react to a psychic giving an unsolicited reading; I was intrigued but not overly anxious about Mandara's alleged vision. I was still reveling in the fact that I had finally shared this secret after twenty-eight years—a secret that was very much at the forefront of my mind, as I often wondered where my sister ended up and what her family life was like. Several times over the years, I had passed women on the street who looked like they could have been related to me and seemed to be the right age, and I'd wondered if one of them was my sister.

What if she never knew she was adopted? Imagine finding out that way, at twenty-eight years old, a forty-two-year-old man comes knocking at your door and says, "Hi, I'm your brother!" I didn't feel like it was my place to stir such a big pot, so I accepted the recommendations I'd received over the years and didn't go searching for her.

When Iris and I went home, we spoke about her surprise over the news that I shared. The topic eventually dwindled and fizzled out over the weekend, and Monday was back to business as usual. That following Monday, I arrived home later in the evening, following my standard Monday night production meeting. It was around ten o'clock as I pulled into my driveway and found Iris in in the garage waiting for me, screaming and emotional.

"Paul, Paul!" she cried, as I barreled toward her. All I thought was that something awful had happened to one of the kids—a fear that can make time stand still.

"Your sister! Your sister!" Iris continued, almost completely incoherent. *Rita?!* I thought in a state of panic, now wondering what had happened to her.

"No, your *other* sister! The one you just told me about on Friday. *She found you!*"

I finally got Iris to calm down and string together a useful sentence. My little sister, Sheila—the one my mother gave away twenty-eight years ago—had found us and was on her way to my sister Rita's place.

It's astounding to think how much your world can be tossed upside down with a single phone call. *What if it was someone from that coffee shop?* I wondered, unable to comprehend the fact that this could all be real, and my little sister had, in fact, found me. My first instinct was to call my lawyer to see what he thought about meeting this woman face-to-face. I had just sold my company in a very public transaction and was uneasy about the potential for exploitation. He advised me to meet her, and provided solace with the reminder that I had, in fact, never revealed this secret until only a few days ago, so how would anyone even have context to build the scam.

As shocked as I was, I got in the car and drove to Rita's house to meet this woman who claimed to be our sister. It was all so unbelievable and nearly impossible to process.

I arrived at Rita's house nervous, excited, confused, and reluctant. I didn't know what to expect or how to move forward, and our family as we knew it was about to change completely. Our lives were about to change completely.

As we waited together for Sheila to arrive, Rita expressed her shock and utter disbelief over the fact that I had known about our other sister this entire time.

"How did you find out?" she asked.

"That night at Uncle Jack's after Mom was taken away in the ambulance. I wasn't really sleeping when he explained everything to you," I replied.

She genuinely had no idea that she wasn't the only one carrying the burden of our family's secret. She also shared, that much like me, she was curious about finding our sister over the years but had been repeatedly advised against doin so by her legal counsel, so she, too, had left it alone.

In a matter of moments, the doorbell rang. Rita and I stood in front of the door holding hands and looking at each other. I finally pulled the door open and saw a couple standing under the porch light: a tearful woman wrapped in a man's arms.

"I found them! I found them!" the woman cried. Within seconds, any questions I had about Sheila being my real sister were gone; she was the spitting image of my mother. We hugged and gathered in Rita's living room for a conversation we'd all been waiting twenty-eight years to have.

She was accompanied by her husband, Gene, a kind and supportive man who was absolutely wonderful to Sheila and our family that night—and for the years to come. Every few moments, I became taken aback once more by the fact that I was sitting across the room from the little sister I had just met.

"How did you find us?!" we asked Sheila.

She regaled us with an unbelievable story about how her parents had told her she'd been adopted at a young age, and she always had the desire to find her birth mother and simply hide behind a nearby tree and look at her. But over the years, Sheila's curiosity never subsided. Sheila also shared that her daughter, Jodie, who'd been born with blonde hair and blue eyes, had health problems that the doctors told her were genetic. This reinvigorated Sheila's determination to find her birth mother, motivated by lifelong curiosity and the added questions about the health conditions her daughter had inherited.

Sheila's birth certificate listed Helen Lane as her mother, Dr. Bratspiss as the delivering doctor, and Brooklyn Hospital as the location of birth. It didn't list my father's name, as he was dead by the time she was born.

Sheila had been told by her family that he'd been killed in the war, but Rita and I corrected that, and shared the details of the night my father died in our home. Rita and I continued to listen in awe as Sheila shared the details of first calling every Helen Lane in Brooklyn—to no avail—and then calling every Dr. Bratspiss listed. Of course, she wouldn't have found my mother since she was remarried by then. But Sheila had a stroke of brilliance and thought maybe the doctor had changed his name from Bratspiss. So, she began calling every Bratspiss in the phone book, asking the voice on the other end of the line if they had any relatives who were doctors in Brooklyn and might have changed their name.

Wouldn't you know it, she found a cousin!

He told her his cousin had an ob-gyn practice in Brooklyn and he had recently changed his name to Dr. Bradford. Sheila made an appointment with him, left her daughter with her mother in New Jersey, and made the trek to Brooklyn. Minutes into her appointment, Sheila explained to Dr. Bradford who she really was. He remembered her instantly and said that he was the one who arranged for her adoption. He shared with Sheila that he remembered the night she was born, and also told her that he'd taken care of Rita for many years.

"Who's Rita?" Sheila asked the doctor.

The doctor had casually handed a bombshell to Sheila, who now knew she had a sister. Cleary, I'd never met Dr. Bradford, since growing up, I had never required the services of an ob-gyn.

Sheila was shocked and excited to find out she had a sister. She begged Dr. Bradford for her contact information, but he said that this was all he could share with her for now. He told Sheila to come back in two weeks, as he needed to think about whether or not it was appropriate to share any more information. He would use this time to think it through and discuss it with his family and attorney.

Two weeks passed, and Sheila returned to Dr. Bradford's office to find that he had decided to share the address he had for my family at the time she was born.

"This is all I can give you for now," Dr. Bradford said, as he explained that he was violating a code in sharing this information, but her tenacity and the effort she had put into finding her family had moved him in such a way, he felt compelled to share the little information he could.

Sheila's next stop was our old apartment building at 268 Linden Boulevard in Brooklyn. She walked five flights to the top floor and began knocking. Door after door, Sheila knocked, introduced herself and explained her situation, but found no one who lived there when my family did. She went to every apartment, on every floor, and finally came to the last door on the bottom floor. Behind that door lived Mrs. McGinn, an elderly Irish woman who definitely lived there when we did.

"You're not Helen's daughter," Mrs. McGinn proclaimed, as Sheila was introducing herself and doing her best to explain her story. "I knew Helen's husband Julius, I knew Rita, I knew Paul, who are you?!"

"Wait—who's Paul?!" Sheila asked.

"Oh, Paul is your brother!" Mrs. McGinn explained.

Sheila had once again been slipped a bombshell wrapped in a simple sentence. She now knew that she had a sister and a brother somewhere out there and was more determined than ever to connect with the family she'd never known.

Since it had been years since Mrs. McGinn saw any of us, she got her daughter Patty on the phone to try and locate one of us. I knew Patty growing up, and I definitely had a little crush on her. Patty told her mother that she hadn't seen me in years and didn't know much other than that I lived in the New York area with my wife and kids.

Armed with this information, Sheila once again hit the phone book and called every Paul Lane listed in Long Island. On her eleventh try, a woman answered, and Sheila began making her way through her story. This woman was Iris.

"Is this the home of Paul Lane?" Sheila asked.

"Who's calling?" Iris retorted. As Sheila began making her way through the story, Iris stopped her.

"I know who you are; just say it! I know you're his sister!"

So, there we were, catching up with our sister and unraveling a secret that has been kept for nearly three decades. This reunion was quite noisy and ended up waking Rita's kids. Within moments, Sheila had met her brother, sister, two nephews, and a niece. It was an overwhelming occasion that none of us would soon forget.

I was glad Sheila had pursued us. As we sat there talking and crying and in awe of the situation, I thanked Sheila for her tenacity in finding us and explained to her that we would be glad to have her in our lives.

Sheila denied that she was born on the thirteenth of April and had grown up celebrating her birthday on the fourteenth. As the story goes, Sheila was born at 11:30 p.m., and my mother begged the doctors to push her listed date of birth to the fourteenth. Since Rita and I were both born on the thirteenth of the month, we all assumed our mother did this as her way of providing Sheila with a shot at a good life; as if being born on the thirteenth of the month was some sort of bad omen, especially given the tragedy and poverty our family was experiencing at the time of Sheila's birth. To this day I still tease Sheila and refuse to celebrate her birthday on the fourteenth. In spite of her insisting that she keep her birthday as the day listed on her birth certificate, I will only send a card or plan a dinner in her honor on the thirteenth. It's our favorite little inside joke that I will never let go of.

But everything would be up to her as to how we would proceed and develop this relationship. I also told Sheila that her mother was still alive and living in Florida.

"Would you like to meet her?" I asked, proposing a plan for the three of us to travel down to Florida, where our mother now lived. Sheila agreed, as meeting her biological mother would be the final piece of this puzzle. We made the arrangements to travel south for what we thought would be the reunion of a lifetime.

Rita arrived in Florida first. I came down a day later, and Sheila was to come the day after that. I had to leave the day Sheila arrived, as I had to go back to work.

The plan was for me to break the news to my mother that Sheila had found us; Rita and I would then have lunch and discuss it all, and the next day, Rita would introduce Sheila upon her arrival.

I entered my mother's living room like an operative on a mission, kissed my mother hello, and sat down to begin a calm yet meticulously planned conversation. Rita was waiting in the next room, accompanied by a doctor in case my mother fainted from the news.

"Isn't this beautiful, Mom?" I remarked, gesturing out the window at the view of sunny Palm Beach and its beautiful homes and perpetual summer scene. "Remember when we were poor and didn't have things like this? Dad wasn't there. You had to give up the baby because things were so tough for us. But look where we are now. Look how far we've come!"

For some reason, I thought if I slipped it smoothly between a few other sentences, my mother wouldn't have much of a reaction. It quickly became evident that this theory didn't apply to dark family secrets coming to light.

"What did you just say?!" she said as soon as the words left my mouth. My mom truly believed that no one knew the secret she carried and was so ashamed of. I calmly explained that I knew, Rita knew, and most of the immediate family knew. I spent the next few minutes calming my mother down, reassuring her that she had nothing to be ashamed of, and that this decision was not something that would ever be held against her.

"And you don't hate me?" she cried in response. For the first time, I saw how much shame and guilt my mother had carried with her all these years having to give her daughter away in a time of great despair. My heart broke for her, and I did my best to reassure her that no one hated her. In fact, we all considered her brave and selfless for making such a hard decision and truly putting the baby's needs first.

My mother's rush of guilt eventually subsided, and she agreed to meet Sheila. Their meeting was cordial, not warm. I could never understand what it must have been like for Sheila to look the woman who had given her up for adoption in the eye and introduce herself. I am quite certain we all had visions of how this would turn out, and the hope of becoming one big happy family.

Sheila learned that she'd only been given up because our father had recently passed away, and our family had been experiencing such difficulty making ends meet after the loss of our breadwinner. But even knowing this, she was never able to get over her resentment for our mother giving her away. It was especially difficult for Sheila to let go of this resentment, given the fact that by the time she'd come into our lives, we were light years away from being the poor Brooklyn family we'd once been. She was picked up in a Rolls Royce at the airport, and it was glaringly obvious to her that all of us had grown to be financially comfortable over the years. Ultimately, Sheila and our mother would never be able to develop a strong relationship; cordial would always be the height of their interactions.

Rita and I were a legendary brother–sister duo, with a powerful bond. Sheila always felt like she was never really a part of my sister and me, and as if she were a perpetual outsider. I have a hard time correcting her. The thing is, nothing bonds people together like times of struggle. In one tragic moment, Rita and I went from constantly annoying each other to partners in struggle, relying on each other to overcome the difficult times we faced growing up. Our struggle is what bonded us, and Sheila wasn't there to share that part of our lives with us. She wound up being the lucky one, living in a home filled with love and having the opportunity to go to summer camps and eventually college. We were simply from different worlds. The tragedy of my father's death and the camaraderie we shared while growing up in poverty was the glue that created such a bond; for a long time, all we had was each other. In many ways, Sheila bore the brunt of this. I did my best to welcome her and treat her like family but couldn't help the fact that Rita and I were close, and Sheila would never be able to share that with us, simply because we were apart for many years.

The boundary that existed between Sheila and Rita and me became more pronounced because of the physical distance between us. Sheila lived deep in New Jersey, while Rita and I lived ten minutes apart on Long Island. I am certain that if we lived closer to each other, visits would have been more frequent. Sheila began feeling like we didn't make as much of an effort to see her as she did to see us and would always remind me that I didn't need a passport to come to Jersey. But I believe Sheila's expectations far outweighed ours, setting her up for us to disappoint her more than once.

Years after being reunited with Sheila, I experienced something very close to a heart attack and was hospitalized. I hate having people around me in the hospital and urged both Rita and Sheila to stay away. Sheila obliged and didn't come, while Rita was hearing none of it. She showed up unannounced and uninvited, to see for herself that her brother was going to be okay. Sheila found out that Rita had come to the hospital, and although it was never our plan to exclude her, it broke her heart. Following this misunderstanding, Sheila made the decision that she wouldn't see us anymore. It had all become too difficult for her, and she thought the best thing she could do would be to remove herself from the situation. This lasted for about a year, when Rita finally took the initiative to reach out. This wasn't the first or last time Sheila had distanced herself, but it was always Rita who brought us back together.

"I'm not letting her go," Rita would insist, as we once again rehashed the relationship we were doing our best to build.

Over the years, the bond between all of us began to grow closer—especially between Sheila and Rita. Sheila would eventually become as much a part of our lives as any sister could be, and I must give her credit for how hard she worked to spend time with us and create a real sense of family.

and Rita is the blonde on the left.

As I write this, I am only a few months past the incredible loss of my sister Rita. Our bond remains unbreakable, and a big piece of me left when Rita passed. Sheila had also grown incredibly close to Rita, and was there with her when she took her last breaths. Outside of my kids, Sheila is now the only immediate family I have left. Perhaps that's why we met—to spend almost four decades becoming brother and sister in order to support each other in our later years. In spite of having lived so long without knowing Sheila, her entrance into our lives was a great addition, and I am grateful for the magic that led to our paths crossing.

As this story unfolded, a wave of negative and even angry responses flooded in from people who had caught wind of my sister appearing in my life again. "How could she do this to you? *To your family?!* Why would you stir the pot like this?" they would ask, lips dripping with judgment and what I perceived as an overreaction to business that concerned no one but my family. However, through these interactions I learned just how surprisingly common adoptions were for this generation. And the hostile reactions I received were merely projections of personal experiences from certain people who had either adopted or given children up for adoption due to poverty. I carried this secret for nearly thirty years, and through its unraveling, I learned that our situation was much more common than I had assumed, and there were countless people walking the same streets I was, carrying the same dark family secret.

The funny thing is, for the past seventeen years, I've had a sneaking suspicion that Sheila may not be the only immediate family I have drifting about. These thoughts first surfaced seventeen years ago, while I was visiting my father's grave. As I approached the spot where my father was buried, I noticed fresh stones had been placed on his gravestone—a Jewish tradition loved ones practice to honor and memorialize their loved ones who have passed on. I scratched my head wondering who could have left these stones there, since most of my immediate family had passed away. For the next seventeen years, and up until the last time I went to my father's grave, fresh rocks were always sitting atop his stone. When my father was still alive, I remember him being quite the ladies' man about town, rarely home. I also remember my parents separating on multiple occasions, prolonging the blocks of time in which he would be absent. Who knows where he was, what he was doing, or who he was doing it with, but I am unable to rule out the idea of his having more children than we knew about. In consideration of that fact and the mysterious rocks that have been consistently placed on his gravestone for nearly two decades, something tells me Sheila may not be the last long-lost family member to show up on my doorstep.

Chapter 8

Bought Out

I CAN'T SAY MY LIFE HAS BEEN A ROLLER COASTER, because that would imply a single track. I'd say my experience on earth so far has been more like a Tilt-A-Whirl: ups and downs in every direction, with no track to help me predict where I'm headed next. By the mid-1970s, I had lost my first wife, was preparing to divorce my second, and had just been found by my younger sister who had been given up for adoption by my mother less than an hour after she'd been born. Amidst this mayhem, I still had a business to run, and I was passionate about building it.

My company, Dobie Originals, had now become Dobie Industries, and was thriving. My partner, Nat Peters, and I not only developed a growing business together from scratch, but we also became great friends during the process. Nat and I were a perfect fit, both as friends and partners. Our skills were complementary, and we operated with mutual respect. It was truly the ideal partnership, and I will be forever grateful for Nat. He was a survivor of the Holocaust who escaped and made his way to America. His work ethic was unmatched, and the way he ran operations and manufacturing was a major factor in our ultimate success. In a few short years, we grew from a two-man operation into a major apparel manufacturing corporation with five production facilities in North Carolina.

By now, Dobie had become a major supplier of childrenswear to all of the big chain retailers, like J.C. Penney, Sears Roebuck, Macy's, Spiegel's, Kmart, and Target, as well as dozens of smaller chains around Manhattan. We developed a reputation for integrity and for supplying quality, well-designed merchandise that aligned with trends and consumer behavior. We also received a tremendous amount of support from banks and other factors, which set the stage for banking opportunities that would seem unfathomable today. Unlike the current world of banking, which is stringent, grueling, and far too automated to feel personal, in those days banks would lend money to businesses based on the rapport between banker and customer. During a casual lunch with my accountant Harvey Jurist, one of the top guys at Clarence Rainess & Company, I casually mentioned that if I could somehow secure a loan for $1 million dollars, I would be able to fulfill a major order for J.C. Penney. It seemed like a lofty idea at best—even a fantasy—and I never thought much of it. But Harvey saw potential and had faith that we had what it took to secure this level of loan.

"Let me try something," Harvey said after a moment of reflection. Within days, we were sitting with the senior vice president of Chemical Bank, who I was told had been a priest prior to changing his career to become a banker. We presented the various reasons why my company was worthy of such a substantial loan. I walked him through the reasons I needed the money and a precise repayment plan. I wrapped up my speech, and sat back, expecting to be laughed out of the room. The banker leaned in and turned to his colleague.

"Give him the money," he said casually.

My jaw was on the table. In spite of not having anywhere near a million dollars' worth of assets, I was able to secure the loan that would give us the opportunity to fulfill the order for J.C. Penney; what a coup this would be for our company!

We continued to grow, thanks to the skills of our designers, manufacturers, and sales teams, and Dobie Industries had risen to the ranks of being relied upon to supply childrenswear to some of the biggest retailers. Our reputation of quality and integrity preceded us, and we began to receive pitches from various companies who wanted to do business with us.

At the time, American Greetings was a greeting card company that was looking to expand into other industries by leveraging their roster of characters. They created a subsidiary company called Those Characters From Cleveland, Inc., and shopped their characters around to major manufacturers, including apparel and toy companies.

One afternoon, a representative from American Greetings came in to show me one of the characters they had designed, which was receiving an exceptional response as far as greeting card sales went. The young character caught my eye instantly. She had red hair and freckles, and I thought she would work perfectly as a logo for our girls' wear.

The character was named Strawberry Shortcake, and I had no idea at the time that she was about to change the track of my professional life.

I was able to negotiate a favorable price for the Strawberry Shortcake license and began adding the images to some of our girls' clothing soon after. The designs and garments went through our standard channels of distribution and began to appear on the shelves of major retailers around the country with the rest of our standard inventory. Within days I began receiving calls from merchants, begging for more of the Strawberry Shortcake apparel. It was flying off the shelves, and people couldn't get enough of it! It began selling faster than we could produce it and was the catalyst that took my business to a new plateau. We no longer had to proactively sell this merchandise; it was selling itself. The retail tables had turned, and unlike the previous lines that I had to go out and pitch to buyers, our Strawberry Shortcake apparel had the buyers racing to us. People I had done business with for my entire career were calling me, eager to acquire another shipment of the Strawberry Shortcake. Everyone from buyers to merchandise managers would call me, excited and frantic, and requested the merchandise as if they were calling in a personal favor.

This relatively small investment I made in an unknown cartoon girl with red hair and freckles wound up making many merchants and me millions of dollars and changed my business forever. To this day, most women over thirty remember the red-headed animated starlet fondly, and perhaps have even owned a Strawberry Shortcake item of clothing or a toy. Everybody loved Strawberry Shortcake.

Through watching the unexpected impact Strawberry Short-cake had on consumers, I discovered the power and potential of licensing in the apparel industry. This newfound approach would become one of the biggest causes of my career success.

During the mid-1970s, consumerism was flourishing, spending was at an all-time high, and mergers and takeovers were a common thing in the apparel industry. But not all of them were successful. Many businesses crumbled soon after the transaction had occurred, and many companies didn't value themselves properly, getting the short end of a devastating deal. Strawberry Shortcake had made quite a splash in the apparel industry, and I had a lot of eyes on my company, but, I wasn't in a hurry to sell or partner. That's not to say I didn't fantasize about one day selling a part of my company and becoming one of those people with a bunch of cash *and* a company, but I wasn't open to just any deal.

I was eventually approached by an accounting firm that was acting on behalf of Cluett, Peabody & Co., a 140-year-old apparel company that got its start making shirts and collars for cowboys at the turn of the century. To this day, their story as one of the pioneers of menswear is told in a permanent exhibit at the Smithsonian. They were a legacy corporation and an industry giant and they owned some of the strongest menswear lines at that time, including Arrow shirts and Gold Toe hosiery. Since the majority of their manufacturing business was geared towards men and boys, they were looking to expand into different demographics. This led them to approaching one of Manhattan's premier accounting firms, to help identify and acquire a top-tier childrenswear company to add to their roster, and they recommended Dobie Industries. This was an opportunity of a lifetime for any small business owner looking to get bought out.

After months of meetings and due diligence, Cluett, Peabody made us an offer to join them. They gave me the option of choosing stocks or cash, and I made the shortsighted mistake of opting for cash, as I was nervous about how risky stocks could be. Had I thought long term, I would have chosen the stock option for many obvious reasons. But I took the cash, and the deal was done. I was proud to be considered a part of the Cluett, Peabody roster. The Dobie brand remained intact and joined the Cluett group of companies as their childrenswear division. I remained the president, and Nat continued to manage the production and supply chain.

I was once again thrown into the deep end of a new challenge, and I will admit, I was terrified. Cluett, Peabody's executive team was a force to be reckoned with, consisting of Ivy League alumni at every level of the company, highly skilled and formally trained in each one of their functions. It was intimidating, to say the least, and I was nervously awaiting the moment when one of the higher-ups would figure out I didn't have the credentials to walk the same hallways as these elite individuals. I felt like a kid in a world of kings, but as long as I was allowed to be in the building, I was committed to building their childrenswear division for *just one more season*, if not more. I signed a two-year conditional contract with Cluett, although that would be the last contract I ever signed with Dobie, even though I would stay there for the next fourteen years.

Being a part of the Cluett, Peabody organization afforded me privileges and conveniences I had never known. I had access to the company's Learjet and a corporate apartment in Olympic Towers to use as needed. In spite of my home life being in continued disarray, my professional life was shaping up quite nicely.

Shortly after the acquisition was finalized, I was asked to prepare a five-year forecast for the division, which was to include financials, budgets, projected revenue, and an overall plan. This

News from Cluett

Cluett, Peabody & Co., Inc.
510 Fifth Avenue
New York, New York 10036
212 930 3000

Alatex Inc.
The Arrow Company
Cluett, Peabody Int'l
Clupak, Inc.
Continental Hosiery Mills

Dobie Originals
Donmoor, Inc.
Duofold, Inc.
Fischer Mills
Glentex

Great Am. Knitting Mills
Halston for Men
Jet Sew
Lady Arrow
Retail Stores Division

RPM Fashions
The Sanforized Company
Saturdays in California
J. Schoeneman
Spring City Knitting Co.

Contact: C. Supplee   930 3033   Release Date: **December 18, 1980**

CLUETT NAMES LANE GROUP EXECUTIVE

Gordon E. Allen, president of Cluett, Peabody & Co., Inc., the large apparel firm, has announced that Paul Lane, president of Dobie Originals, a Cluett Division, will become group executive for children's wear on January 1, 1981. In this new post he will be responsible for the future development of Cluett's growing boys' and girls' apparel business. He will supervise the operations of Donmoor, Inc., a national boyswear brand, and Dobie Originals, which markets young girls' sportswear. He will remain as president of Dobie.

"Cluett entered the children's wear market in 1978," Allen commented, "and this move puts a senior executive in position to devote full time to developing substantial growth in both branded and unbranded lines. Paul Lane was co-founder of Dobie Originals in 1960 and will continue as its active head."

Donmoor, a long-established boyswear brand (since 1897), remains under the direction of Richard Frankfort as president. Along with the Donmoor boys' brand, sold through department and specialty stores, Donmoor has recently introduced a line of girls' wear under the Sweet Fancy brand.

Dobie Originals markets young girls' sportswear to major chains, as well as to specialty and department stores, where the Dobie Originals brand includes popular priced active sportswear for girls aged three to eleven.

-0-

Press release from Cluett, announcing
that I would become the group executive for childrenswear.

proved to be quite the challenge for me, because in those days, longevity was making it through the next fiscal year. Life in my industry was best portrayed in the Oscar-winning movie *Save the Tiger,* a 1973 drama about the clothing manufacturing business, starring Jack Lemmon. The movie's most famous quote, "Just one more season," resonated heavily throughout my career, and was always what we were all striving for in the business—just one more season. How was I supposed to put together a five-year projection?

This is it, I thought. I had convinced myself that this would be the moment that I would be revealed as a phony and asked to never return. But I decided I would go down swinging and assembled a team of my key people: accountants, production managers, sales executives, and other specialists to help me put together a document I had never even heard of, let alone prepared. We set up a war room in the corporate suite, and for the next several days, we took a deep dive into the numbers and compiled our projections as best we could. I took this document to the board of directors but noticed other division leaders were present with much thicker dossiers in their hands.

Shit, I thought, looking down at our twenty-five-page attempt at a forecast. Another wave of doubt washed over me as I found myself once again convinced that I was potentially embarking on professional failure. Nervous sweat dripped down my back as I handed in what I considered to be a flimsy forecast document and began presenting its parts. Nervous yet composed, I spent ninety minutes walking the Board members through the facets of my division, how much money it would require, and how successful we expected it to be each year for five years to come. I spent the rest of that day completely unsure as to how my presentation had been received and whether or not I would be deemed fit to continue. I returned to my office and later that afternoon, and our chairman, Henry Henley, called me. I was expecting to be told to pack my things and go, but instead, he thanked me for providing such a succinct and straightforward plan. He made a joke about how he was far too used to one-hundred-page dossiers, long-winded speeches, and far too much fluff. I'd pulled it off and quickly gained the respect of the executives and my colleagues. I also became quite the proponent of the five-year plan, and over the years, I would request them from my division managers.

I gained the trust I needed to be left to my own devices and run my division, which was off to a strong start. The doubts that stemmed from my lack of education and humble beginnings lingered; however, Nat and I hit the ground running, and Dobie continued to grow bigger by the day. I attribute much of my success in this era and for years to come to the fact that I started from scratch and had to learn and perform nearly every aspect of the clothing business, from design to development to every administrative task you can imagine. I've had my hands on every facet of the clothing manufacturing business at some point or another throughout my career, which helped me not only streamline my process, but also relate to each individual employee through my intimate understanding of their role.

My first major move as a corporate executive would be to expand our reach into the childrenswear market by acquiring Donmoore: another childrenswear company but one that focused mainly on boys' clothing. It was the perfect complement to Dobie's existing operation, which mainly designed and sold girls' clothing. Following this acquisition, I was named the group executive of this roster of Cluett companies, and my role continued to expand rapidly. As Cluett, Peabody continued to increase their market share, they kept handing me more responsibilities. I was always intimidated by large corporations, but found comfort at Cluett, and I was flattered by how I was being treated, and how much responsibility I was being entrusted with. I was approached to develop their womenswear arm. We launched several brands that were solely for women, including Lady Arrow—the women's division of Arrow shirts—and the repurposing of our existing designer line, Ron Chereskin. It performed so well amongst men, we had designers come in and launch a women's line. The reception was outstanding, and my division was growing by the day. The last addition to my roster of companies came shortly after we launched the womenswear division. I was assigned to manage Six Continents, the company that facilitated and provided overseas labor for our various brands.

I've always stuck to the theory that my whole business was taking a piece of clothing that had a front, back, and two sleeves, and finding ways to make it interesting. I had not forgotten how Strawberry Shortcake had catapulted my business to a new plateau, and I was constantly on the lookout for interesting characters and licensing opportunities. My status as a rookie quickly dissolved, and for the next fourteen years, I remained in the ranks of Cluett, Peabody and the clothing industry as a whole, working with Olympic athletes, beloved children's characters, and Hollywood megastars. My journey culminated with the discovery of one the most successful children's character of all time—a goofy purple dinosaur with a theme song that is permanently etched on the minds of millions.

Chapter 9

Lifeline

AMIDST A GROWING CAREER AND THE WHIRLWIND of recovering from the loss of my wife and starting over, I managed to stumble into a philanthropic endeavor that would wind up being a very important and beloved part of my life for the next twenty-five years. It began with a chance encounter on a flight heading to Paris with my family in tow. Soon after I sat down, I engaged in a war of seatbacks and personal space with the passenger in front of me. Frustrated, I recommended that we stand up and have a chat about getting through the entire flight peacefully. The situation diffused quite quickly after the other passenger and I realized the seat was broken. We had a good laugh and introduced our families to each other, since we were all traveling together. I learned the couple's names were Jay and Ethel Wyner, and they were traveling to Paris with their two teenage daughters. We talked about our travels and where we lived in New York City, and quickly realized that our families lived rather close to each other on Long Island. As the plane landed, we exchanged contact information and agreed to keep in touch since we were nearly neighbors with several mutual friends.

For months to come, I would see the Wyners socially and continued to build a friendship. On one occasion, Ethel shared with me her lifelong passion project, which was the Lifeline Center for Child Development. It was a small school in Queens, designed to educate and care for children who faced learning disabilities and other mental health challenges like autism, Asperger's, and ADHD. The school was staffed with teachers, caregivers, and specialists whose ultimate goal was to work with each student on a special track that would hopefully lead them to being integrated into a regular school, or what they referred to as "*mainlining.*"

I fell in love with the program; it seemed like a wonderful initiative and a few of our neighbors sat on their board. I always had a sneaking suspicion that Ethel was nudging me to get involved, and after a few visits to the school, that's exactly what I did.

Everyone loved the program Dr. Wyner and her team had created for these children, who were in a constant state of risk. The teachers were motherly, and truly cared for the children's learning and development. There was 360 degrees of care—from trained educators to health care professionals who specialized in mental health. It really was quite the endeavor, truly ahead of its time.

I served as a board member for the following three years, working with other participating board members on the business side of things and developing successful fundraising initiatives. I recruited several powerful friends of mine, including Deborah Grafton, who was VP of Kmart at the time, Betty Vitaly, who was the merchandise manager of Lerner Shops; and several powerful executives and attorneys. I was determined to build this school into a larger institution, and always had an affection for the children whose success in life depended heavily on this program. After three years of being an active and passionate board member, I was voted in as president.

As Ethel continued to build the curriculum and specialized care programs for the students of Lifeline, I focused on fundraising initiatives with the ultimate goal of building a larger school that would help hundreds of children with special needs.

We raised money through golf tournaments, movie nights, and other formal events, but our bread and butter was the Candyland Ball: our annual fundraiser, which brought out New York City's professional elite and other A-listers with deep pockets. The event was held in the ballroom of the Pierre Hotel, and would take place every first Saturday of December for the next twenty-two years. Over four hundred people attended, dressed in their finest, and each year we would invite a guest of honor to be recognized for their service to the community and hopefully bring some friends who liked to make large donations. I learned quickly that political figures were not the best choice for guests of honor, as they seemed to be more concerned about their own soapbox and acquiring voter support and cash for their campaigns.

In spite of this experience, one year, our board picked Meade Esposito—a Brooklyn Democratic leader—to be the guest of honor for that year's Candyland Ball. But as time passed, and the date of the gala got closer, my team began to realize that Esposito hadn't done the legwork we generally require from our guest of honor, including publicizing the event and getting their network to buy tickets.

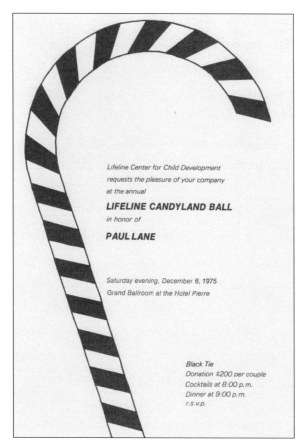

Lifeline Center for Child Development
requests the pleasure of your company
at the annual

LIFELINE CANDYLAND BALL
in honor of

PAUL LANE

Saturday evening, December 6, 1975
Grand Ballroom at the Hotel Pierre

Black Tie
Donation $200 per couple
Cocktails at 8:00 p.m.
Dinner at 9:00 p.m.
r.s.v.p.

A flyer from one of our Candyland Ball
fundraisers where I was the guest of honor.

We were frantic, as it looked like we were about to blow our budget on hosting an empty ballroom. Since Esposito wasn't returning our calls, Ethel and I decided to travel to Brooklyn to talk to him in hopes of getting some last-minute commitment. We arrived at his office, a dimly lit den of secondhand cigarette smoke filled with people waiting to ask for his benevolence. His secretary waved us in, and we entered his office and walked toward the seats on the outside of his desk.

"What can I do for you folks?" he asked from behind his desk, with a big cigar hanging out of his mouth.

"Mr. Esposito, we have a problem," I said, and began to explain that he had accepted the invitation to Lifeline's Candyland Ball, and we were counting on him to not only show up, but also invite his network and help us raise funds. I shared with him that our event was in trouble, and it didn't seem like he was holding up his end of the bargain as this year's guest of honor.

Esposito seemed confused, and it quickly became clear that both the folks who had extended and those who had accepted this invitation had not done their part. Not only had our event never made it to his calendar, he was scheduled to be in Kansas that day for the Democratic National Convention.

"I'm sorry, folks," Esposito began, after confirming he wouldn't even be in the city on the day of the ball. "There has been a terrible mistake, and I just can't make it."

My appeal was passionate. I could tell that Esposito was trying to shoo me out of his office, but I had no intention of leaving. I was determined to save the event, and since I was in his office already, I figured I'd take one last shot at conveying the importance of this event and our organization in general. I went into more detail about what we did at the center, how many kids we'd helped, and how integral it was that this event was a success. He listened intently, and in the blink of an eye, I watched his whole demeanor change. He warmed up to us; my soapbox speech about Lifeline had definitely gotten his attention.

Within seconds, he buzzed his secretary into his office and requested a plane back to New York City on the day of the event. He also informed her that he needed 250 people to show up at this event and gave her the event details to deploy to invitees and potential guests.

I was shocked and filled with delight in watching this man save our gala in a matter of moments. I thanked him and promised that he would be treated as if this event were his bar mitzvah.

The night was a huge success, and also the first time we had the children from our school perform. About twenty of our students arrived at the Pierre by bus, and sang songs and dance routines they had learned and perfected over the semester, and our guests loved it. There wasn't a dry eye in the house. It was very moving and a powerful demonstration of how effective our teachers, caregivers, and therapists were. The evening was a success!

Several years later, I knew I was on the path to retirement, and I wanted to leave my mark on the Lifeline Center before passing on the torch to the next board president. We had over $3 million in the bank from the past few years of fundraising, and I felt we were ready to build a bigger and better facility. Even though we had the funds ready to go, the challenge was in the organization. I kept making requests to the board to form a building committee to oversee the development of the new facility, but busy schedules were unable to align, and that endeavor proved to be impossible. Frustrated and determined to get this project rolling, Ethel and I asked for the board's permission to take the reins, and with our guarantee that we would keep them informed along the way, the board gave Ethel and me the green light.

I was ecstatic about the opportunity to develop the entire facility from the ground up. Armed with a $3 million budget and the input of teachers, doctors, and other experts, I began working with an architect to design the new Lifeline Center, which would be built in Queens. This would be the biggest challenge I'd ever faced, because I wanted to make sure the building was thoughtfully designed and considered the unique needs of our students. Before breaking ground, we spent hours meeting with teachers and experts to determine what the kids needed the most. A plan was formed, and several months later, the new facility was built and opened. Everybody was thrilled with the result, from students to teachers to the families. What was once a modest, functional schoolhouse was now two buildings on three acres, offering an array of facilities and amenities, including a swimming pool.

When I started at Lifeline, there were six students, and by the time I left, the student population was over 250 students from infants to twelfth graders. Since the new facility offered a much higher level of functionality than the old, smaller school, Ethel and her staff were able to embark on various projects to diversify the programs and improve the care they offered. They also spent time visiting children at home and developing plans and programs for the students when they were outside the school and at home to support and essentially expedite their success.

After twenty-five years of service with Lifeline, I stepped down because I was moving out of New York. My son Curtis took over as president, and I remained attached to the school through a seat on the board.

Year after year, Lifeline continues to help students with learning difficulties and other special needs to grow, develop, and eventually graduate into the regular school system. The building is still intact, and a roster of on-site experts continue to offer customized clinical services and educational programs to help students develop and thrive. And while, sadly, Ethel Wyner passed away in 2010, her legacy is strong, and the programs that she singlehandedly engineered with very few resources continue to grow and flourish. Some of her ideas and concepts have even permeated regular schools across New York in classrooms designed to support children with special needs and behavioral concerns.

Throughout my entire career, Lifeline remained the endeavor that I was most fond of. Donating money to various causes is a great way to give back, but there is something very powerful about getting involved and having the opportunity to see the difference in a child as they progress. I am grateful to have had this experience and proud that the school continues to fulfill its mission.

Chapter 10

Third Time's a Charm

Most parents can agree that life comes at you hard once your kids are born, but some have a much smoother ride than others. I consider my children the three greatest accomplishments of my life. As I reflect on my life as a father to two sons and one daughter, I am grateful for them and proud of the people they have grown to be. I may not have been a perfect father, but they rode the roller coaster that was my life right alongside me and came out on the other side as successful professionals and wonderful parents to children of their own.

I always knew Curtis would be a success in business, as he displayed an unwavering work ethic from the time he was old enough to grasp the concept of responsibility. My favorite story about Curtis comes from when he was a teenager on Long Island, working at a bagel shop part time. A massive snowstorm had covered the East Coast in snow and essentially paralyzed New York City, but Curtis woke up every morning at 4:00 a.m. and made the freezing-cold, snowy trek to the bagel shop to start his

109

shift. Even the owners took the day off, but Curtis was adamant about showing up for work. He remained steadfast and focused in this way throughout his life and managed to work his way into the upper echelon of Manhattan's business elite.

Jeffrey is three years older than Curtis and marches to the beat of a much different drum. He has gravitated toward a simpler and more intellectual side of life. He loves music and the outdoors, has never been intrigued by the hustle and bustle of New York City, and doesn't seem to care about keeping up with the Joneses.

My third child is my daughter, Tracey. There is something extra special about the bond between a father and a daughter. Today, she has a successful business of her own in the fashion industry and is married to a great guy. As you may recall from a previous chapter, Tracey's childhood was anything but run-of-the-mill, and it felt like I boarded a roller coaster ride from the moment I brought her home from the hospital.

Me with my three wonderful kids, all grown up.
Tracey is to the left and Curtis then Jeffrey to the right.

In the early '80s I was an executive in the retail industry with a career that had already far exceeded my expectations, and my involvement with Lifeline had captured my heart and much of my free time. But my personal life was back in shambles. I had just initiated my divorce, was living in the Kitano Hotel on Park Avenue, and once again found myself picking up the pieces with no clue what was next for my family. I was in the midst of becoming a single father of two grown sons and a teenaged daughter, and thanks to new divorce-settlement legislation, I was about to hand over the majority of everything I'd worked for to a woman I was anything but fond of. Business was good, but when it came to my personal life, it was always something.

Dating was the last thing on my mind when I met Brenda. She was a strikingly beautiful advertising executive who worked with my division at Cluett, developing advertising campaigns and planning presentations around the work we were doing. I definitely noticed her—anybody would—but thought nothing of it, as she was engaged to my friend Sid Dulman. Brenda is the person who was in my office presenting a new line of toys when I got the call from my frantic friend whose daughter had just taken her life. The shock and despair of the moment caused me to jump out of my seat, do my best to politely excuse myself, and rush out of there to get to my friend as soon as possible. Not knowing the facts, Brenda assumed that I had hated her presentation until I was able to clear it up with the sad truth about my friend's daughter.

While Brenda was undeniably charming and gorgeous, I only thought of her as a colleague. She was intelligent and known throughout the company as competent, creative, and reliable. One afternoon, she and her team were packing up after a presentation about licensing the Playskool Toys as one of the properties we would consider working with. As they were walking out, I casually inquired about my friend and Brenda's fiancé.

"How's Sid?" I asked, and the room fell eerily silent. I knew right away that I had asked the wrong question and was quietly informed that they had called off the engagement because Sid didn't want to take over the responsibility of her two young sons. I felt bad about bringing it up but was immediately intrigued and invited her for lunch a short while later.

"I think we could both use a friend," I said to her in an attempt to break the ice at the beginning of our lunch. My marriage had just fallen apart, and she was a young widow whose new engagement had just ended. Life for both of us was abysmal, and thus I thought it would be a bit more enjoyable to suffer together. We spent more time together, and I quickly saw her as a friend and confidante. But soon enough, I inevitably fell head over heels in love.

The whole encounter changed my life around. I never thought I would feel love like this again, but I did. We had an unbelievable amount of tragedy in common, which gave us both a unique perspective and understanding of each other that strengthened our bond.

By this time, I had moved into an apartment at the Lombardy Hotel, which seemed to be the headquarters for the who's who of folks waiting on their divorces to finalize. Richard Burton, Rex Harrison, and Bette Davis, as well as the not-so-famous Paul Lane took up residency there to wait for the ink to be dry on our divorce decrees and the chance at liberation.

I informed the chairman of Cluett that Brenda and I were in a relationship and suggested that he could perhaps assign someone else to take over my responsibilities of buying advertising since it was Brenda who would be presenting the purchase options. I wanted to avoid questions and conflict and having my romantic life affect my professional reputation. But the Chairman knew both of us, and Brenda's work, and trusted us to handle our relationship professionally and continue working together.

I would have married Brenda after the first six months of dating her, but we were in a unique situation. It took two years for my divorce to be finalized, and then a few more years of doing what we could to maintain a normal life for our kids. At the time, it was important to Brenda that she keep her sons on their track in New Jersey. Their father was quite a prominent man before his sudden and tragic passing, and the family believed that their children had a bright future following in their father's high-profile footsteps. Her two sons, John and Chaz, were going to school in New Jersey, where Brenda lived at the time, and I had moved out of the Lombardy and back into an apartment in the city in the Park Belvedere building at 79th and Columbus, which was only an up-and-coming neighborhood at the time. Brenda would stay with me some nights, and some weekends I would go out and see her. You know a New York City guy is in love when he's willing to travel to New Jersey to see his lady, and that's exactly what I did throughout our eight years of courtship.

The first time I went to New Jersey to visit Brenda, I was introduced to an aggressive, controlling, and seemingly mean-spirited woman. Unfortunately, this was Brenda's mother, who lived with her in the house Brenda had acquired. It was clear that Brenda's mother ran the home like a Nazi concentration camp: everyone and everything was meticulously clean, and Brenda's sons were fed and provided with the essentials, but the mother would routinely abuse Brenda both verbally and physically and berate the boys in ways they never deserved. It was a toxic environment that I didn't want to be a part of, except for the fact that I was in love with Brenda and knew I would have to find a way to make this work.

I learned quickly through my visits that Brenda had a very hard upbringing at the hands of her mother, and by the nuns at a school she went had attended. Much of her parenting was based on what she perceived as godliness, but in real life it was abuse. However, unlike Brenda's brother John, who managed to escape his mother's iron clasp, Brenda was fiercely loyal to her, doted on her, and took care of her every need in spite of being treated so horribly.

When I walked into her home for the very first time, Brenda's mother was barking at her within minutes. This outburst was simply due to the fact that she hated the way Brenda was slicing carrots while preparing our dinner. I was appalled at how ferociously she spoke to Brenda in front me—a brand-new guest and possible suitor—but she berated her without any shame or a blink of an eye.

The actions of her mother had a permanent effect on her and her sons. Even Brenda's father—who seemed to be a good man—was overwhelmed by the tyrant that he married. No matter how Brenda succeeded or the grades she got in school, her mother would continue to berate her. I believe that on some level Brenda's mom was jealous of her. And this was passed on to the boys. She assumed the role of a violent dictator, and the boys were made to fall in line as if they were soldiers. I tried tirelessly to get Brenda to agree to an alternative for her mother, which included getting her out of the house and away from the boys, but the combination of her mother's aggression and Brenda's loyalty enabled Brenda's mother to stay in the house and continue being the tyrant she truly was.

Brenda's kindness and loyalty towards her mother ultimately forbade her from even considering the option of moving her out. So, for the next eight years, we fought against the adversity of our situation by traveling, commuting, compromising, and doing what we had to in order to keep our relationship going strong whilst living in neighboring states. We did what we could to be together and did our best to provide a loving and relatively normal life for our kids along the way. John and Chaz did take a while to warm up to me, as they were used to the gentle kindness of their mother, and I was stricter when it came to my expectations of both my children and Brenda's. They also had strong ties to their father, who had died suddenly in a car crash several years prior. But once they realized that I loved their mom very much and I was in it for the long haul, I felt a shift in their attitudes toward me and we finally began to feel like family.

Brenda and I got along famously, and she truly became my partner in everything. We were united in so many deep ways, including the fact that my first wife and her first husband had died very young. Unlike my second wife, who was outwardly jealous of the fact that I held on tightly to my memories of Joan, Brenda had a unique perspective and encouraged me to continue to honor her memory in any way I needed to. As the last of our kids went off to college, Brenda sold her home and moved in with me in the city. Her mother was forced to return to her own home—which she had the entire time, yet she had insisted on staying with Brenda and tormenting her. Our time was spent in the city or at my second home, which was a boat that was docked in the Hamptons during the summer and down in Florida during the winter.

Me with Brenda.

After our years of courtship and commuting, the timing was finally right, and we got married in the Rainbow Room at Rockefeller Center on December 15, 1990. When the justice of the peace pronounced us husband and wife, our friends and family went wild, and it was a beautiful, long-awaited celebration. As much as I'd thought that when it came to having bad luck at my wedding, I couldn't top getting hit by a bus on the night of my marriage to Iris, I was wrong. My bad wedding luck wasn't over, and toward the end of the party, I felt a sharp pain in my chest and was rushed to the hospital.

Of course, I thought. Happiness always seemed to get blown up by something, and here I was having a heart attack on the night I'd finally married Brenda. I was relieved to hear that it was not, in fact, a heart attack, but rather a bad reaction I was having that was caused by mixing one of my medications and alcohol. I returned home exhausted, far too tired to carry Brenda over the threshold. Thankfully, my son Jeffrey stayed with us in the hospital and helped us get home. Jeffrey was always witty with a sharp sense of humor, and wasted no time lifting Brenda up and carrying her over the threshold on my behalf since I was in no shape to pull it off. We still laugh about that moment.

Brenda and I have always shared a deep bond based on being parents, experiencing similar tragedies, and overcoming hardships. But while we are such a great match, life throughout our marriage threw us a few terrible curve balls we had to work hard at over-coming. The first of several tragedies came when Brenda's son Chaz was diagnosed with lupus when he was twenty-four years old. At the time, my knowledge of lupus was limited, and all I knew about it was that it was a relatively manageable disease. Sadly, Chaz had a rare form of the disease, and he wound up losing his battle after six years, in March 2002. I've seen a lot of terrible things in my lifetime, but few can compare to watching a mother lose her son. I was shattered, but doing my best to be strong for Brenda in the wake of the worst thing that could ever happen to a parent. What made it even worse was this was the second child Brenda had lost, as years before, her two-and-a-half-month-old son died of health complications.

After Chaz's death, Brenda and I stayed in touch with his wife

117

and now widow, Lisa. She and Chaz never had the chance to have kids, so we no longer had any familial ties to her, but we loved Lisa and Lisa adored Brenda so much, and it would have been an awful gesture to abandon her after Chaz's sudden passing. We were united in a tragedy we had all individually experienced far too early in life, and Lisa had become an important and indelible part of our family. Brenda encouraged her to join a support group, where she eventually met and married a wonderful man named Richard with whom she later had two children.

To this day, I regret not going to Lisa and Richard's wedding, but I had such a difficult time with everything because I loved Chaz so much. Over the years, I grew to love and accept Richard, and nowadays, their kids refer to Brenda and me as "Grandma" and "Grandpa," and from time to time there is so much love between all of us that Lisa and Richard refer to us as "Mom" and "Dad." Their daughter, Alessandria, is an accomplished equestrian, and they stay with us during the Hampton Classic. We love hosting them; Richard is a dream guest—cooking, cleaning, and taking care of everybody. Brenda and I also spend time with them at their timeshare in Cabo San Lucas, as well as in their home in New Jersey. To me, they are as much a part of my family as the rest of my children and grandchildren, and Chaz's presence remains with us at every step.

Brenda's other son, John, chose a woman who was nothing like Lisa, and actually displayed similarities to his grandmother, Brenda's mother. From the day I met her, I knew in my heart she was not a good choice for John, as she silenced our attempts at conversation so she could fill the air with stories about herself and her family. Perhaps John felt most at home being dominated by a controlling, nasty woman since that's what he grew up with, and he sure managed to find those qualities in his wife.

We were never invited over to see the children or have any contact with them, all because of John's wife shutting us out. She was mean-spirited, and the only contact we continue to have with the kids is through cards, gifts, and phone calls sent and initiated by Brenda. It's constantly devastating to be shut out of the lives of our family members, but her cruelty won't allow for a healthier scenario.

I will never forget one of my last ugly encounters with John's wife. It was shortly after Chaz died, and Brenda and I brought John a box of Chaz's belongings that we thought he would like to have. We arrived at the house with the box, and before anyone had the chance to open it up and see what was inside, she was already scoffing at it.

"I don't want that in my house! Get that shit out of here!" she barked at us. I was furious, but Brenda being the gentle person she was, quietly suggested we leave, and so we did, taking the box with us. We have never been back to their house.

In the months leading up to Chaz's passing, my daughter, Tracey, was pregnant with her second son, Andrew, who was born soon after Chaz died. Although he was carried to full term, Andrew was born with a rare genetic defect that was life-threatening and he was essentially brain-dead. The devastation was overwhelming. It was hard to breathe or think or accept this terrible information, but like anything else, it simply had to be dealt with. I thought there was a certain cruelty on the part of the hospital, leaving Tracey to remain in the nursery ward alongside the rest of the mothers who were having their babies handed to them. It was awful to be there, surrounded by healthy babies while we sat there riddled with sadness and worry. After speaking with the doctors, I was tasked with the job of convincing Tracey and her husband, Lou, to remove Andrew from life support and let nature take its devastating course. They agreed, and two days after Andrew was born, I sat with Tracey and Lou as we took turns holding this tiny baby who was literally dying in our arms. I knew I needed to stay strong for them, but the moment I was able to sneak away, I ran across the street to Central Park in the middle of the night and sobbed in devastation and frustration over the fact that tragedy seemed to haunt my family perpetually. A few short hours later, Andrew passed away.

It took a couple of years for some level of normalcy to return to our lives after the deaths of Chaz and Andrew, but as we all finally felt like we could breathe again, another tragedy struck. As Tracey returned home from a vacation with her family, she arrived to find her apartment building on 72nd Street engulfed in flames. In the blink of an eye, they lost everything. Thankfully, no one was hurt in the fire. "Stuff" can always be replaced, and our family came together to make sure Tracey, Lou, and the kids were able to start over with everything they needed.

After the dust settled, and we were all doing our best to move forward, I received a frantic call from Tracey while I was sitting at dinner with a friend in Boca Raton. Tracey screamed and cried into the phone, and I ran straight to the airport. She had been diagnosed with cancer.

Cancer.

The word I had spent a horrible few years ducking, dodging, and hiding from my first wife was back to haunt me again. Tracey had a unique form of cancer in her nostril, known as neuroblastoma.

The original suggestion for surgery was to open the scalp and go through the brain; reminiscent of the procedure my Joan had had more than forty years prior. But thankfully, a network of medical connections courtesy of my son Curtis, who was established in the medical community, enabled Tracey to receive world-class treatment. Curtis connected us to a specialist at the Hospital of the University of Pennsylvania, who was able to remove the tumor and its margins via her nostril. Tracey then entered into radiation treatment for six months, and I am grateful to say she has been cancer-free ever since.

Throughout all of the tragedy, Brenda and I became one another's rock, and it wound up bringing us closer together. I was so grateful to have found an ideal partner who had lived a life that had given her a unique understanding of what I had gone through before her, and what we faced together.

I was starting to believe that "normal' is not a long-term setting for my family, but it had been quite some time since our last tragedy.

It was 1995, life seemed to be going fine, and I was in the market for a new car. I ended up finding what I was looking for at a BMW dealership in Fort Lauderdale, and was ready to cut a check for the cost of the entire car.

"You don't need to pay all of that upfront, Mr. Lane; we can check your credit and go over financing options, since interest is currently only 1 percent," the saleswoman told me.

Check my credit? I was completely unfamiliar with this concept. I had become accustomed to working with bankers in my professional life but had never encountered a need for a personal loan, let alone gone through the process of running a credit report on myself. Curious but confident in my personal finances, I asked her to run a report. What came back was astonishing.

"Mr. Lane, based on your credit report, we can't offer you any financing options," the saleswoman explained, nervously holding a printout of my credit report. "It says you have more than twenty credit cards here, and—"

"What?!" I interrupted her, shocked and certain there had to be a mistake. "I only have one credit card," I explained, gesturing to my wallet.

This is how I found out about Brenda's horrible disease, which came in the form of a spending addiction. It's not in my nature to be suspicious, so I had never thought to comb through our finances in such a way, but after learning about this I began to dig deeper. I sadly learned that after we got married, Brenda had signed my name on a slew of credit card applications, and this seemed to be a secret that everyone except me knew about.

I felt betrayed and began to consider getting out. I confronted Brenda about it and she was crushed. She didn't try to hide anything and owned up to everything she had done over the years: the credit cards, the shopping trips, and using small amounts of money to maintain the minimum balance and keep creditors off her back. She pleaded with me not to go, and to help her get treated for this disease that had clearly grown out of hand.

I began studying addiction and learning more about the effects it can have on a person. I started to see it as a sickness just like cancer, and was willing to put everything I had into helping Brenda beat hers. I helped her get the care she needed, from rehab to therapy sessions. We also unpacked the idea that perhaps it was the years of abuse that had caused her self-esteem to eventually deplete, and the short-term high from buying something new had become especially profound. Who knows? I didn't understand what was happening, but I loved her and believed that with the right therapy and treatment, she would snap out of it. I guess you can say I am forever tenacious when it comes to saving my loved ones, and while I was unable to save Joan from her disease, I had every intention of fighting and winning the war against Brenda's addiction.

I believe that there is no cure for addiction, only maintenance strategies for keeping it at bay. For years, and up until this day, it has been a difficult task that included many relapses, disappointments, and troubling incidents of letting this disease win, but I have remained committed to her throughout the process.

Prior to this experience, I wasn't familiar with addiction and what it took to overcome it. Even after years of treatment and therapy sessions, we continue to worry about the potential for a relapse. The lesson here is that not all diseases are curable, but with the right treatment and commitment to fighting back, addiction can be controlled.

My lawyer and I challenged the credit card companies and got them to reverse all the charges since, ultimately, my signature had been forged. It took me a couple of years, but I won every single claim. We are still together and have since been through a handful of tragedies, but with the same determination and courage to go on. She is still my rock, and I'm still hers. On paper, three wives can raise an eyebrow or two from time to time, but this is my path, and I'm continuing along it as best I can.

Addiction elicits judgment and blaming, whilst cancer elicits pity. Addressing the mental health concerns of myself and my loved ones has been a key factor in my life since the days I served in the psych wards of army hospitals during the Korean War. To this day, these issues remain stigmatized, and blame, unfortunately, seems to be placed on folks whose brains have simply been wired differently and who are prone to having difficulty facing life the way our society expects us to. I learned about how difficult it is to cope with addiction through Brenda's bravery in admitting that she had a problem. All too often, an unfair blame is placed on people who suffer from addictions, and they are made out to be perpetrators as opposed to the victims they really are. I learned to consider cancer and addiction in the same manner—as illnesses that one doesn't choose but must face and treat accordingly. I am proud of Brenda for allowing me to share her story in hopes that perhaps someone will read it who is facing the same demons and see that they are not alone in the struggle and there is, in fact, a way out.

In this world of good, bad, and everything in between, the courage to go on was granted to me by something I'll never know. I am by no means a hero. I simply believe that no matter the situation, you must face it and keep fighting for yourself, your goals, and those you love.

Chapter 11

Care Bears, Olympic Golds and the Road to Hollywood

Back to work. Cluett, Peabody was a tradition-ally conservative company, and my tenure as group executive was mainly driven by developing creative concepts that challenged the industry and boosted sales. My experience with Strawberry Short-cake allowed me to see firsthand how powerful an impact the right characters had on the childrenswear market, and I was able to grow my business through strategic partnerships with artists and designers, and with movie studios, as well as intriguing licensing opportunities.

I met Carole MacGillvray during my time building Strawberry Shortcake. She came up from managing a toy store in Massachu-setts to becoming the vice president of General Mills, the company who designed toys for Kenner Toys. I always liked working with her because she was sharp, with a keen eye for picking the right characters to use for building merchandise lines.

125

Soon after I signed on with Cluett, Carole excitedly presented a collection of children's characters for me to consider licensing. They were a group of ten cartoon bears who spread kindness and fought evil with love. Since bears were typically brown, she had the brilliant idea to make them all different colors to represent their different emotions and personalities. Each Care Bear represented a different method of kindness one can practice in order to spread cheer and happiness. There was Bedtime Bear, Birthday Bear, Cheer Bear, Friend Bear, Funshine Bear, Good Luck Bear, Grumpy Bear, Love-a-Lot Bear, Tenderheart Bear, and Wish Bear. I was quickly intrigued, and by the end of the day I had acquired the license to the Care Bears—characters that still resonate fondly with most people over thirty all over the globe.

These bears were endearing, fun, and colorful, and their story-line made a huge splash, and they were starting to become revered globally. We began including images of the Care Bears on some of our apparel, and retailers couldn't keep it on the shelves. They were an instant hit and another great success for Dobie and for Cluett, Peabody as a whole. We were invited to be a part of the Macy's Thanksgiving Day Parade. The organizers insisted that the Bears should march, and I was invited to join the march. My team and I came up with the idea to hide me in one of the suits, and I would walk in the parade as Tenderheart Bear. The day of the parade, I was walking in my full Tenderheart Bear costume, except for the head, and a young boy ran up to me to say hello.

"Hi, Mr. Care Bear!" he said with excitement, smiling up at me.

"Hi there! How are you?" I replied with a chuckle, but someone from Kenner Toys quickly nudged me and reminded me that Care Bears don't talk, and I promptly shut up.

126

I walked behind the scenes of the parade until I found the float I would ride on for the day. I was hoisted up onto the float's platform in my bulky Tenderheart Bear costume, and a cherry picker was used to lift and place the head of the Tenderheart Bear costume onto my head and off we went down Central Park West toward Macy's. It was a thrilling morning to be a part of the Thanksgiving Day Parade. Through a small screen in the head of the Tenderheart Bear costume, I was able to watch as crowds of people cheered us on and kids screamed for the Care Bears as if we were the Beatles. It was a real scene—and a family affair, as my wife, Brenda, and daughter, Tracey, were part of the Strawberry Shortcake float that rode behind the Care Bears.

Dobie employees got such a kick out of my involvement with the Care Bears and the fact that I was marching in the parade that they created a contest amongst my employees to see who could guess which bear Mr. Lane was. Whoever guessed correctly would win a trip to Disney World. It took quite a while until someone finally guessed it correctly … perhaps I wasn't thought of as much of a "Tenderheart." Who knows? It might be tough to imagine, but these charming little bears wound up being lovable creatures that have stayed consistently famous for years and years. Our lines were flying off the shelves, and my division in Cluett, Peabody became the top choice for entertainment companies looking to venture into the world of apparel and merchandise.

I had a great eye for picking the right characters to license, but also managed to mistakenly pass on a few great opportunities. One afternoon, a guy from one of the design companies we worked with called me to pitch a group of four mutant turtles dressed as samurai swordsmen who knew martial arts and inhabited the sewers of New York City. They were names after Renaissance artists and were guided through life by their Sensei, a giant rat. I was fearful as to how it would appeal to a child's taste, and felt that the turtles didn't really fit in with the rest of my roster of characters, and wound up passing. Fast-forward thirty-eight years, and the Teenage Mutant Ninja Turtles are still a major hit and a permanent reminder that I had my share of bad calls.

It was now the summer of 1984, and the Olympics were taking the world stage live from Los Angeles. It was the first time in fifty-two years that the Summer Olympics would take place in the United States, and the US-versus-Russia rivalry had reached a palpable level due to the Cold War.

The women's gymnastics final was that year's hot ticket, pitting American Mary Lou Retton against Ecaterina Szabo from Romania. Mary Lou had been injured just prior to the event, and the fact that she could even compete at this point was a miracle. In a dramatic performance, Mary Lou scored a perfect 10 on the vault, securing her place as the all-around gold medal winner, but the Russian judge challenged it. In those days, gymnasts had two chances at their vault, and the judges would consider the best score from either jump. Mary Lou had already scored a perfect 10 on her first vault, but in a display of sheer athleticism, she opted to do it a second time to prove she deserved the perfect score. Just like that, she flew over the vault, twisting and flipping, and stuck the landing perfectly. She proudly earned herself a perfect 10 for the second time in a row and secured the medal. She also became the first woman from outside of Eastern Europe to win the all-around gold, and instantly became "America's Sweetheart."

Her manager, John Traetta, was a friend of mine, and soon

after she won the gold, he reached out to see if Dobie would be interested in acquiring the license for her likeness as well as the opportunity to develop a line of children's activewear geared toward young female athletes and athletic girls.

It seemed like a no-brainer at the time, as she was the face of athleticism and American pride, and her face was all over television stations, magazines, newspapers, and Wheaties boxes in grocery stores across the country. Working with Mary Lou Retton was a whirlwind. I have never met someone so young with such a powerful presence.

She was calm, bright, and comfortable in any setting. Everyone loved Mary Lou Retton, and she was gracious with each and every person she encountered. I would fly with her and her brother—who acted as her chaperone—all over the country to make personal appearances, and she was treated like royalty everywhere we went. We always needed police and security due to overwhelming crowd sizes and the frenzies she would cause. Mary Lou and I once went to the UPMC Children's Hospital of Pittsburgh, and I remember her greeting each child she encountered with kindness and candor; I've truly never met anyone like her. She was an absolute delight to work with. She was able to relate to anyone, from CEOs to toddlers, and everyone just adored her. For a sixteen-year-old girl, her personality and demeanor were so impressive. It wasn't the kind of thing that you can train someone to have. Some people are just special in that way.

All the major retailers were soliciting me to arrange for a personal appearance with her, and she was perpetually enthusiastic, gracious, and accommodating. When J.C. Penney held a meeting in San Diego, over 1,800 store managers as well as the company's

129

Me with Mary Lou as she is signing her contract to work with Dobie Industries. Her manager is behind me, with his hand on my back and the VP of Dobie Industries is standing behind her to the left.

executive team assembled for the major event. I worked with Henry Scott on an idea to bring Mary Lou down as the surprise part of the introduction of the merchandise, since we had agreed that J.C. Penney would be the first retailer to receive our products. Just after Henry finished his regular presentation, he introduced the brand-new Mary Lou Retton line of activewear. The crowd erupted in excitement over the news that they would be the first retailers to introduce the line.

"I've got another surprise for you," he said with a smirk, and the stage curtains opened up to reveal a large cake. In a flash, Mary Lou Retton jumped right out of it with the same vigor as when she jumped over the vault in her gold-medal-winning performance. The room went wild, and the managers were hooting, hollering, and banging on the tables with excitement over the fact that Mary Lou was there. Even the highest-level executives and chairpersons were humbled in her presence, excitedly requesting autographs and pictures.

Me to the left of Mary Lou and the President of J.C.
Penney children's store to the right. This was after signing
her contract before we introduced the new clothing line.

Shortly after, we were invited to Sears Roebuck's 100th anniversary in Chicago at the prestigious Sears Tower. The guest list was an impressive roster of celebrities, top executives, and professional athletes. Mary Lou was an instant hit, and everyone was anxious to meet her. By now we were fielding invites to major events around the country from folks who were desperate to have Mary Lou attend their event. One of the most exciting invites we received was facilitated by one of the big department stores in Louisville, Kentucky. They invited us to make an appearance at their store and then show up for the Kentucky Derby. Mary Lou and I agreed that it would be a fun trip and something of a break for us all to go down. We had heard of the exciting events that took place around the Derby as well as the Southern hospitality of the folks in Kentucky, and we were delighted to attend, especially since none of us had ever been to the Derby. We got the company jet and took Mary Lou; her brother; Brenda; John Traetta; and his wife, Mary Jane, to Louisville, Kentucky for three days. Everyone was thrilled to have us!

The night before the Derby, we were invited to a dinner where they served unforgettable barbecue accompanied by fresh corn on the cob. As I bit into the corn, my entire front tooth broke off and stayed in the cob! I panicked … how was I supposed to attend the Derby the next day, with all those cameras and me standing beside Mary Lou with a hole where my tooth should have been?! Brenda and I were beside ourselves. Fortunately, the chairman of the store that invited us all down arranged for me to get in with a dentist at seven o'clock the next morning. To my great relief, he saved my dignity and appearance for the day. I was grateful to learn that he had no intention of accepting payment from me since he was so excited about the fact that I had brought Mary Lou to his city.

On the day of the race, a motorcade of police officers showed up at the hotel to accompany us to the Derby. The police officer at the front of the pack got off his motorcycle and walked over to our limo to introduce himself.

"Mr. Lane, it would be a great honor to get Miss Retton's

autograph," the officer said to me.

"Sure," I replied, and Mary Lou happily obliged, as she always did.

I returned with the autograph and handed it to the officer.

"I can't thank you enough, so I'm going to show you how we really do it in Kentucky!"

The officer returned to his motorcycle and signaled to the other officers, idling in a row in front of our hotel. Within seconds of our limo pulling out of the hotel driveway and onto the street, we had a full police motorcade with cops on bikes on either side of our car, escorting us to the Derby. It was an exhilarating experience that none of us would soon forget.

We arrived at the Derby as guests of Kentucky's Governor Collins. The governor approached me herself and asked for an autograph and picture, and naturally Mary Lou obliged. Governor Collins thanked Mary Lou for the honor she brought to the state and the pride she had brought to the country. When the Derby was over, she called me over to her box to thank me for bringing Mary Lou. She was so thrilled about all of it, she bestowed upon me the honor of becoming a Kentucky Colonel—the highest honor given by the state to civilians in recognition of major accomplishments or significant service to the community, the state, or the country.

After the successful development of several character-driven childrenswear lines and the frenzy caused by Mary Lou Retton, I shifted my focus back to Hollywood.

I learned about a forthcoming collaboration between Disney and Spielberg: _Who Framed Roger Rabbit_, a one-of-a-kind production that combined live action with animation. This was the first such film, and it was generating an enormous buzz. I was then invited to Studio City, Los Angeles, and found myself on the sprawling grounds of Spielberg's lot. We were invited into a private screening with other executives, and it was fascinating to watch Bob Hoskins shooting scenes in which he was communicating with a static object that acted as the placeholder for the sultry Jessica Rabbit, who would be animated into the scene in post-production. The movie includes a parody of Mae West's famous line: "Is that a pistol in your pocket or are you just happy to see me?"

There was so much buzz around this creation. A meeting followed the screening, where we would learn more about the production and the opportunities that came with it. I saw the potential of the whimsy and magic of Roger Rabbit, and stuck around to advocate for Dobie to acquire the license. In the middle of the meeting, Jeffrey Katzenberg, a dynamic executive who oversaw licensing and merchandising projects, appeared in front of us. He started talking about the project and noticed that I was there with Brad Globe, so he shifted the conversation to licensing. In the blink of an eye, he explained that they were specifically interested in debuting the Roger Rabbit merchandise in a major retail store like Kmart, instead of being spread thinly throughout a collection of different stores.

Just like that, the meeting was over. We all left the lot, and I drove to a restaurant nearby called Nate 'n Al, a popular spot for celebrities and folks in the movie business. I walked in and, as if by a stroke of dumb luck, there sat the executive vice president of Kmart, Debbie Grafton, who was in charge of the company's apparel division. I rushed over, thrilled to run into her, of all people, at this exact moment. We greeted each other, and I explained to her that I'd just left the studio, and there was an exciting opportunity on the table. I began trying to persuade her to join us for a meeting the next day.

"How's 9:00 a.m. tomorrow morning?" I asked, doing my best to lock in the meeting. She agreed to let me pick her up then. And in less than twenty-four hours I was able to deliver the exact deal that the Disney and Spielberg execs were hoping for, as a result of sheer serendipity.

At the meeting, Debbie was impressed with the production. Katzenberg stopped by to greet her and thank her for coming, and was clearly impressed that we were able to bring her in. We ended up acquiring the exclusive rights to Roger Rabbit. Although the character Roger Rabbit was geared toward adults, I thought that the movie would cause such a buzz that everyone would be interested in having a piece of the merchandise—including children. The movie opened at the legendary Radio City

One of the advertisements Dobie Industries created to promote Roger Rabbit as our official licensee.

Music Hall, and was attended by many of the major retailers who were interested in being part of the *Roger Rabbit* buzz. The film received rave reviews, and the whole thing was considered a success. Since its release, there have been many movies done in a similar style, but *Roger Rabbit* remains the original and most beloved of its kind.

I would go on to obtain licenses and produce merchandise for a roster of major motion pictures, including *Dick Tracy* and *Robin Hood: Prince of Thieves*. It was an exciting time, because each project brought me onto the movie set, and I was able to see some of Hollywood's icons at work. It was fascinating!

My career offered me the chance to develop some of the most recognizable brands and characters in childrenswear to this day. But I had no clue that I was just a few years shy of stumbling onto the character that would define my entire career: a goofy purple dinosaur with a theme song that would have kids hypnotized worldwide.

Chapter 12

Fast Times on the High Seas

The Pleasure Lane burning down in the middle of the ocean.

As I STOOD SOBBING ON THE DECK OF MY FRIEND'S rescue boat, clutching Brenda as we watched my prized sixty-foot yacht burn to a soggy crisp in the Atlantic Ocean ten miles off shore, I started to think that perhaps I should have stuck to golf.

137

Once again, something I had grown to love so much was now flanked by tragedy, but little did I know this was just the beginning of a nautical adventure that would wind up taking me halfway across the world.

* * *

I picked up a passion for boating shortly after I threw in the towel on my originally favored leisure activity, golf. After losing a tournament to a man I couldn't stand, I couldn't, for the life of me, find a reason to continue with an activity that was meant to be relaxing but actually caused me more stress than my workweek. Perhaps I hated the fact that I might not be the greatest golfer out there. Who knows, but either way I wanted out. After shoving my golf clubs deep in the back of my garage and vowing never to take a swing again, I knew I needed to find a replacement activity to help me unwind and enjoy what little free time I had.

It was the mid-1970s, I was in my early forties, and by this time I had the means to invest in something fun. Perhaps the fact that I lived out on Long Island caused me to stumble naturally onto boating, but soon after I accepted the fact that I would never tour with the PGA, I purchased my first boat. She was a beautiful twenty-two-foot SeaRay Cruiser I named "The Simple Seamen," and it was love at first cruise. Back then, you didn't require special credentials to operate a boat, but I enrolled in the Power Squadrons boating school anyway to hone my skills and become a confident captain. I quickly fell in love with it, and boating soon became a way of life—and my boat, a second home. I was still married to Iris at the time, and together with our daughter, we would sail around the Long Island Sound and New York City, exploring every port in between. I set my sights on something bigger, and soon acquired a thirty-six-foot boat that I brought to Montauk and treated like a summer home. It was truly my release, and I loved my boat like it was a member of our family.

Iris never took a liking to boating the same way I did, and had made the threat more than once that either the boat goes or she goes. Needless to say, a few short years later, my bitter and lengthy divorce from her was well underway. I truly was grateful to have the option of escaping out to my boat whenever I wanted. You can't put a price on escaping from the hell that engulfs your home once divorce proceedings commence. It was ugly, and my goal became to spend as little time around that woman as I could. I would escape to the boat by myself every chance I could, and was happy to have a way to enjoy the peace and serenity of life on the water in solitude.

As my divorce finally came to a close, I was once again looking to graduate to a larger boat. I decided on a forty-seven-foot Pacemaker that I would name the Pleasure Lane, and could not have been more excited about getting out on the water with my family and friends and taking even longer trips up and down the coastal United States. Since Brenda and I began dating shortly after my divorce, she was soon invited along on the trips and became like my first mate (only much better-looking than the ones I had gotten used to), traveling with me everywhere and living a great life on the water.

For the first time, I set out to take the boat on the ten-day journey from New York down to Miami—a very common route for snowbirds and avid boaters from the northern states. I hired a captain, who spent ten days with me teaching me the ins and outs of boating on longer journeys in order to get my skills up, so I'd be confident to begin making this journey myself. We ended up leaving the boat in Florida at the end of that season, and it became like a vacation home.

It was now the end of summer in 1997, and I was taking the boat from New York back to Florida after spending the season traveling around New York, the Hamptons, and New England with friends and family. By now, I had completed the journey from New York to Miami several times, and had become quite familiar with the route. Before our ultimate departure, Brenda and I docked in Atlantic City for the night so we could fuel up and rest. This was a normal route for many boaters, and I ended up running into Rolly, captain of a ninety-footer and a familiar face I would cross paths with periodically throughout the season. I always liked knowing that someone I knew was close by, and always suggested that we employ some form of the buddy system, as there was often a long stretch of water between ports. I relied on the buddy system often, during more trips than I can count.

Oddly enough, the next morning was the day that Princess Diana was killed in a tragic accident. Brenda and I shared our shock at this devastating news as we were gassing up and departing for the journey. I had hired a young man named Mike to help me on the boat, and he joined us that morning with his dog and off we went. It was a perfect day to be on the water. Mike was puttering around somewhere on the boat, Brenda was on the lower deck reading, and I was up on the bridge, thinking to myself how much I loved this boat and the upgrades and gadgets I planned on buying once we'd made it to Florida. I really did care for this boat as if it were a lady I was courting, and I was always looking for ways to improve it.

"Paul, I smell smoke," Brenda yelled to me from down below, as I was lost in the bliss of being out on the water on such a perfect day.

I quickly snapped back into reality, stopped the boat immediately, and ran downstairs.

"What are you talking about?" I cried, hoping she was wrong but confirming she wasn't, as the unmistakable smell of smoke made its way to my nostrils.

I followed the smell and made my way to its source: the engine room. I made the fatal mistake of opening up its door to see for myself, and then quickly closing it after seeing the smoke and relatively tiny fire that had started. Almost immediately, the boat's safety system activated, loud alarms started to sound, and foam began shooting into the smoke-filled engine room.

At the time, the fire was still a relatively minor one and probably would have remained a small, smoldering flame that would have only left smoke damage in its limited path. However, when I ran back to the wheelhouse, I was unable to shut off the starboard engine, which caused air pressure that began sucking the foam out of the fuel room and out the back of the engine.

"Mayday! Mayday!" I yelled, shouting my name, location, and situation into the ship's radio, hoping someone would hear it and help me.

We were ten miles off the coast of Ocean City, Maryland, and the coast guard wasn't far away. They responded almost immediately to my calls for help, but informed me that their forty-two-foot rescue boat was in for routine servicing, and that they were working on deploying a smaller boat of emergency responders to come and help us.

I always say that on that day, Murphy hopped on my boat, because truly, everything that could go wrong was going wrong. The flames seemed to be growing by the minute, and I had just now been informed by the Coast Guard that the smaller boat had broken down on its way to us, and their men were working on the problem and still trying to get to us. By this time, they had also informed us that they had deployed a helicopter for an emergency rescue. Even recalling the comedy of errors now, it feels surreal, but unfortunately this was our reality at the time, and rescue options were dwindling fast.

"Pleasure Lane, Pleasure Lane, I hear you!" said a voice through my radio. It was Rolly, my travel mate who'd left Atlantic City at the same time I had. My mayday calls had reached his radio, and he assured me he was on his way to me as fast as he could get there. By this time, I had a helicopter, a coast guard rescue boat, and now a fellow boater heading in our direction. It was just a matter of who was able to get to us first.

"Get off that boat! Get off that boat!" he said. "It's going to explode!"

Rolly beat the coast guard and pulled up alongside my boat as Brenda, Mike, his dog, and I rushed down to the swimming deck.

"Jump in!" Rolly urged, as he began dropping a ladder into the water. *No damn way*, I thought, aware of the number of sharks in those waters as well as the fact that I had no interest in swimming up to a ladder that was next to the boat's huge propellers.

"Bump me!" I yelled back. We both threw out our boat fenders and Rolly reversed into my boat, leaving only a few seconds for all of us to jump from my boat into his. We were safe, but only had the clothes on our backs and the American Express card I had tossed

142

into my pocket after we set sail, in case I needed to stop and buy filters along the way.

We spent the next four hours on the deck of Rolly's boat, watching, through tear-filled eyes, as the boat burned to a crisp. It was a devastating sight, made worse by the realization that the majority of our most important and prized possessions were on that boat—some of them irreplaceable. Other rescue boats began circling mine in order to submerge it with huge waves and ultimately capsize it. The last image I have of this boat resembled nothing but a floating, ashy raft with a perfectly intact refrigerator. With one final wave, the Atlantic Ocean swallowed the Pleasure Lane, and I shuddered and turned toward shore, heartbroken. Rolly docked his boat in the port at Ocean City, and we were greeted by a large crowd, including reporters who had gathered to watch the boat burn and sink. Even though it happened ten miles out, the flames burned so ferociously that you could see them from the shores of Ocean City. We answered the reporters' questions through tears and sobs, and called friends and family to confirm our safety.

Rolly was only the captain of the boat he was driving, but thankfully that night he managed to call the owner and get his permission for Brenda, Mike, and me to sleep on his boat so we could get sorted out in the morning. He readily agreed given the circumstances. One of the locals was kind enough to let us sleep on his boat that night, and the next day we made our way to the airport with only what we were wearing and the credit card I had in my pocket. Once we arrived in Miami, I began making a list of everything that was lost in the fire. It became like an insurmountable inventory of my entire life, as we were traveling for such a lengthy period of time, we basically had packed up the majority of our belongings that weren't furniture and were heading to Florida for the rest of the year. I had just had a birthday party, and had a literal boatload of beautiful gifts from friends and family, not to mention all of my office stuff and paperwork I would need while spending the winter in Florida. It was a disaster of epic proportions, and the loss was so great.

Within a day, detectives were at my door to interview me and inform me that Navy divers were currently inspecting the capsized boat that was now at the bottom of the sea, to determine the cause of the fire. I knew the real reason they were there was to check if this was a planned arson for the purpose of getting an insurance payout, which I learned is the case in nearly 70 percent of luxury boat fires. Between my story to the detectives and the evidence gathered by the divers, the fire was deemed a legitimate catastrophe, and I was able to make a claim with my insurance.

Within days, an insurance agent showed up on my doorstep with a bucket of suspicions. The list of lost items I had submitted was lengthy and full of luxury items, including my gifts, a set of golf clubs, and a black-tie tuxedo and ball gown Brenda and I brought with us to wear, which we had first worn to a tango festival months earlier with our friends on the way up to New York. At first, the agent gave me one big eye roll and inquired as to how I could expect her to believe such great loss was actually the case. But thankfully, I was able to collect a decade's worth of credit card receipts from AmEx, as well as the receipts from my friends who'd bought me the birthday gifts, and even a picture of Brenda and me from the Tango Festival dressed in our formal wear, with the date stamp proving that we would have had these clothes with us on the boat. I was able to build a proper claim. I also, as a rule, simply don't believe in scamming insurance companies. People inflate their claims all the time and the rest of us have to pay for it. I refuse to participate in such entitled thievery.

My claim was airtight, and the agent walked away signing off on a 100 percent reimbursement on every item I lost. The insurance company had ninety days to pay me out; on the eighty-ninth day, I received the check, and on the ninety-first day they dropped me from the policy.

With an enormous check in hand, I went to the next scheduled boat show to get myself back on the water. I was way too in love with it to give it up after one measly fire. I attended a luxury boat show in Miami, and there I found the sexiest boat I'd ever seen in my life. It was a sixty-foot Fairline handcrafted in England. The interior was smaller than the Pleasure Lane, but the design and details were so luxurious that I had to have it.

It's not uncommon for new boats to be challenging in the beginning, and I definitely experienced a rocky start with this one—from shutting down spontaneously to the time when I was unable to stop, and wound up bumping into a few boats that were docked at a marina in Marathon, Florida. Their customer service was excellent, and they sent technicians every time to fix the boat at no cost to me, but there just never seemed to be a solution for the perpetual issues I was having at that time.

I planned a trip off the coast of Florida just after technicians flew into Miami and spent two weeks fixing and detailing the boat, assuring me that it was perfect and ready to ride. I told them that I like to do night runs and I'm often with my family, and urged them to reassure me that it was in top shape and ready for the water. They assured me it was, and off I went with my family on the boat to visit my sister Rita. We made it there safely, but on the way back, the boat once again shut down spontaneously, and at that moment, I had had it. I managed to limp back to shore on one engine I'd somehow gotten started and called the company the next day instructing them to come collect their boat and that I would see them in court.

Since boats are hard to insure, I wasn't sure what the outcome would be. But luckily for me, the company had an office in South Carolina, so I was able to sue them in an American court. We had enough evidence of the boat not living up to its standard, and their lawyer in South Carolina ended up calling the company's executives and urging them to settle before going to court in order to avoid paying additional legal fees on both sides. They obliged and offered me a full refund, but I just wanted the damn boat! So they agreed to construct a new boat for me from scratch, which would be ready for pickup in Europe in a few months.

In the meantime, the company worked tirelessly to fix up my previous boat, taking months to rebuild everything and get it to a state of perfection. After lengthy testing and quality assurance, they deemed it sea-ready and put it back on the market, since my new boat was already under construction. The boat ended up getting bought by Celine Dion as a birthday gift for her now-late husband, René. Since I had the ear of the boating company anyway, and she wasn't far from where I was in Florida, I convinced them to let me deliver it to her myself. They obliged, and I wound up driving the boat, over to her estate in Jupiter, meeting her and her entire family, and being a part of the surprise. Everyone was lovely, and it was quite the experience! Admittedly,

I was still in love with this boat and seeing it in perfect condition made it hard to give up. But I gave Celine the keys, wished her a successful surprise, and told her to enjoy the best boat I'd ever had, before I went on my way.

Months passed, and my boat was ready for pickup from the factory in England. The agreement was that I would spend three weeks driving it around the English Channel to make sure everything was in working order before they shipped it back to the US. During the time we were there, Brenda and I stayed in the beautiful little town of Chichester on the southern coast of England. Most people think of England as only London, but this quaint little village was beautiful, sunny, and spacious. It was charming, and the coast overall was stunning, so as the weeks went on, we found ourselves having the time of our lives! I kept extending the trip by a week … and then another week … and I soon realized that I just didn't want to leave. Everything about our lives was so different, and I wasn't done exploring. The boating company paid me out the money it would have cost to ship the boat to the US, and we were off to explore the rest of Europe via the Mediterranean. I still remember fondly how ballsy this decision was, especially since we had only packed enough to stay for three weeks! It was also another moment of reflection at how far I'd come from being a kid in Brooklyn, scraping to get by. Not a moment of this journey went unappreciated.

We left England and traveled to Spain, spending time in Mallorca and finally settling in the little town of Alcúdia. Every day was an adventure, the weather was perfect, and Brenda looked as beautiful as could be under the glow of the ever-present Spanish sun. We then decided to leave Spain, and travel through France, but on our way there, we encountered a heavy mistral, which is a dry hurricane where the winds come off the mountains across the Mediterranean. We had to keep stopping along the way, and what should have been a one-day trip turned into four. We stopped in to a tiny port in the small French town of La Ciotat. Brenda and I both knew enough French to get by, and I figured it would be a fun and interesting adventure in a place unknown to us. I also needed to gas up the boat, so this stop made sense.

The port was filled with rowboats and small fishing boats, and I wound up drawing some attention from the locals when they saw us pull in. Next to the small fishing boats and rowboats that were docked there, our Fairline looked like the Queen Mary! I asked the manager of the marina if they accept credit cards, and as she said yes, I began filling my tank—which ultimately cost me over $4,000. I pulled out my card and handed it to her, and she looked at me, confused. In French, she explained to me that they don't take American credit cards, and I would need to find another form of payment. I had American and Spanish currency onboard, plus a check, but none of it would suffice. She was demanding payment in French francs, and pulled my boating papers so I would be unable to flee the scene.

I started to become worried about what the future held, and visions from movies like *Devil's Island* and *Papillon* danced through my head. She promptly called the police, and within minutes, one of the most handsome men I had ever seen in uniform approached me to explain that she was just the manager, and not to worry, we could work it out with the owner in the morning. The officer was also so enthralled by my boat, he went home to collect his wife and kids so they could come see it.

We spent the night on our boat in the port, and when the morning came, the owner greeted us and reiterated that he was only willing to accept French francs. Images from *Devil's Island* were getting stronger, and now my worries were completely heightened. The police offered to escort me to the mayor's office to sort it all out. The mayor could do nothing to help me, but sent me to the local bank for further guidance.

In my limited French, I explained the story and that money was not a problem; I just needed to get $4,000 from my American credit card to pay for my gas. They couldn't authorize it, and said they needed to call their offices in Paris to complete the transaction. They said they needed an hour for everything, so Brenda and I, along with a few new friends we had made during this whole ordeal, ventured over to a local café to kill time as we waited to hear my fate.

An hour passed, and I returned to the bank, only to find out that my request had been denied.

"I'm sorry, Mr. Lane; there's nothing we can do," the bank manager informed me, with a look of concern on his face. Or maybe it was disgust due to the assumption that I was trying to scam my way into some free gas—who knows. My worry had now peaked, and I began thinking that I might actually end up having to make a run for it. I grabbed the phone to call my bank, frantic and ready to make demands.

"Mr. Lane, we're glad you called us," said an American voice through the phone. "We just caught someone trying to use your card in a small town in France, so we shut it down."

"That was me!" I exclaimed, and walked the agent through my ordeal. In a matter of minutes, my card was reactivated and the bank was able to give me the cash to pay the marina. I grabbed Brenda's hand with glee and we ran back to the docks, forked over the cash, and pulled out of that port with the speed of a bank robber fleeing the scene.

This was one of the most nerve-racking of our adventures, but definitely not the most exciting.

Brenda and I then took the boat and traveled through Saint-Tropez and I fell in love. I would have made it my permanent port in Europe, but quickly learned that the waiting list to rent a dock slip was thirteen years. So, off we went to Cannes, just as the film festival was happening. In a stroke of luck, I remembered that my good pal Stan Lotwin had made a name for himself as a top entertainment lawyer, and he was able to arrange tickets for us to every screening at the Palais—a jaw-dropping venue and centerpiece of the entire festival.

Since it was last minute, I had our trusted mate Glenn help me arrange the next available rental car to drive to this sprawling palace. Dressed in the one and only fancy outfit we each had with us on the boat, Brenda and I pulled up to the Palais, which had a long set of grand stairs leading up to its entrance. Uniformed guards lined one side of the stairs, and a mob of paparazzi lined the other. Glenn, graciously pretending to be our driver, pulled up and stopped the sedan amidst the melee and kindly got out to open the car door like a true pretend chauffeur would. As Brenda and I got out, the paparazzi ran over to us and asked me to quietly step aside so they could get a picture.

"Mademoiselle Deneuve! *Ms. Deneuve!*" they called in Brenda's direction, and I grinned proudly as I realized that they all thought she was French starlet Catherine Deneuve.

Night after night, we attended films with a star-studded crowd, but since we only had one formal outfit each, we had to get creative. Brenda made due by wearing a different scarf over the same black cocktail dress to mix it up, and I woke up extra early each day to hand-wash my dress shirt. We made it work for ten days, and it all turned out to be quite the experience.

This was also the night of the very first Victoria's Secret fashion show, which we were given tickets to. We wound up in a dining room next to the likes of Gregory Peck, Elton John, Joan Rivers, Liz Taylor, and a bevy of American and French celebrities. Joan Rivers was also staying in our hotel, and we ran into her enough times that we wound up getting friendly enough with her to crack a few jokes about marriage and divorce. It was quite the scene of beautiful people dressed in their best and celebrating the film festival.

During one evening of glitz and glamour following the day's film screenings, Brenda, I, and the rest of the attendees flooded a ballroom for one of the after parties. I remember a woman walking around the party completely naked, except for the mesh net that draped over her and a pair of heels. I was in the midst of averting my eyes when we locked eyes and she made her way toward me.

"Paul!" she exclaimed, and I was just as confused as I was curious. I pieced together the fact that she was married to a friend of mine who owned a restaurant in South Beach; at the same time, I felt a hot wave turn my face red. I'm not usually one to blush, but standing in the middle of a crowded party talking to a woman wearing nothing but a net had me as red as a lobster.

Brenda and I did our best to act like we fit into this scene, but really, we were just two starry-eyed kids in awe of their surroundings. It was truly a lap of luxury I had never before and (never after) experienced, and one of the most memorable experiences of my life. I would have never wound up there if it weren't for my boat burning to a soggy crisp off the shores of Maryland.

I had come a long way from the rickety little rowboat I'd had as a kid that I used to paddle around tiny streams in parks around New York City. My life had become a fairy tale that I never sought nor believed could happen. What was supposed to be a three-week trip to the southern coast of England wound up being a two-year-long journey through Europe, stopping at almost sixty ports along the way and only going home during the winters. We traveled all along the French coast, taking in the sites of the south of France and exploring beautiful towns like Villefranche.

The Italian coast was just as breathtaking, and together, Brenda and I visited all of Italy's major ports, from Sardinia to Capri and everywhere in between, including Ventimiglia—the mecca of counterfeit brands. American tourists seemed to flock there to stock up on knock-off purses and leathers, and it was fun to be in the middle of this odd retail frenzy. The mountainous scenery and beautiful villages looked like paintings. Together, Brenda and I experienced the most interesting, exciting, and unexpectedly adventurous life neither of us could have ever imagined, with plenty of visits from friends and family along the way.

Cruel reality often has a way of yanking you away from fun. While this whirlwind adventure was getting more exciting by the day, the journey was not without its fair share of devastation. My sister Rita's son Steven had always been my hero. He was born with a rare condition that affected the use of his arms and legs, but he overcame it and eventually thrived. While I was in France, lost in the fun and excitement, I received word from my son Curtis that Steven had died suddenly due to a heart attack. He was in his fifties. My heart broke for my sister and her family, and I was on the next flight to New York.

This would be the first in a string of tragedies that haunted me during my time boating in Europe. There is a legend in our family that states that everyone should be wary when I travel, because tragedy strikes whenever I go away.

The next jolt of devastating news wasn't far behind. During a cab ride from Venice to Rome, as I prepared to join a cruise ship for a trip up the Mediterranean, I received a call from my son who let me know that my sister Rita's son Alan had lost his battle with cancer. Last we spoke, Alan—a successful doctor beloved by our family—had been fighting the cancer and seemed to be making improvements, but in an instant, everything changed. I rerouted the cab to the airport and was in New York City by that night.

This wouldn't be the last tragedy that riddled my boating years with tremendous pain. On another occasion, I had flown home to Palm Beach to visit my sister Rita's husband, Marty, who was in the hospital fighting his own cancer. We knew the cancer was advanced, but he looked quite well and was in good spirits by the time I was ready to leave Palm Beach and return to the boat. On the final day of my visit, Rita drove Brenda and me to the airport to see us off as we prepared to fly back to Europe. As I kissed my sister goodbye and walked toward the ticket counter, I heard a bloodcurdling cry. I turned around to the sight of my sister screaming and fainting onto the floor. I rushed over to her and held her in my arms as she came to, sobbing and choking out the news that Marty had succumbed to the cancer in his hospital bed just a few miles from the airport.

To this very day, I still get chills thinking of the look of horror on my sister's face as her worst fear became a reality.

At the end of the second year, we felt that we had seen enough, so we put the boat on a freighter and shipped it to Florida. We continued for another few seasons traveling up and down the East Coast of America, until my family convinced me to trade in my big boat for a smaller day boat and a house in the Hamptons. Throughout the next few years, I would experience a handful of life-altering health scares, and my family finally convinced me that it was time to retire from my boating life.

Retirement is always difficult for active people who are passionate about what they do, but boating ultimately provided an exciting transition from a busy work life into my retirement. My home office in Miami overlooks the gorgeous yachts docked on Williams Island, and I often look down on them and reminisce on my incredible travels. I am grateful for each and every moment I was able to be on the water, but less excited to report that I have once again decided to fill my leisure time with golf. I'm still not up to par on the golf course, and as the sign hanging in my office says, "It takes a lot of balls to golf the way I do." Let's just say, I miss my boating days with all my heart.

Chapter 13

Just One More Season

Whenever I reminisce on the years I spent manufacturing clothing, I always go back to the Jack Lemmon movie *Save the Tiger*, which was shot and released in the mid-1970s and is currently available on Netflix, for anyone interested. The story is about a day in the life of Jack Lemmon's character, Harry Stoner, as he does his best to navigate the competitive and risky world of retail. While my experience in the clothing business was much different than Stoner's, I could always relate to him as a person. Stoner was a sharp-dressed man who loved his business, and he and his colleagues were doing whatever was necessary to keep theirs afloat. Whenever I think about this movie, these words always come to mind: "Just one more season!"—a phrase that the characters would decree throughout the movie, as they worked tirelessly to come up with the next merchandising idea. I, too, was perpetually on the lookout for the next great market need.

That's all anyone in the retail business did: look for gaps in the marketplace that they could fill with products and services. What

155

would be the next thing to fly off the shelves? What would be the next Strawberry Shortcake? And while Stoner and his cohorts wound up having to burn down their factory, our company had a much different ending. Ultimately, the movie was an exaggerated depiction of how challenging the manufacturing industry could really be, and for some strange reason, it has made a lasting impact on me. I always carried the fear of looking over my shoulder and seeing one of our factories burning. Thankfully, that would never be the case.

The function of licensing is merely one element in the life cycle of a product. Take the monstrous success of Strawberry Shortcake for example—a cute little character that was originally designed to appear on greeting cards. It all started because American Greetings had an original cast of characters that appeared on their greeting cards but knew that a simple greeting card would most likely never spark a global phenomenon. So, they wanted to repurpose some of these greeting card characters into other products in hopes of generating new revenue. They created a new division called Those Characters From Cleveland, which was essentially the team that went out and presented their line of characters to other industries in hopes of developing them into a lineup of successful retail items, like toys and clothes.

The team at American Greetings knew that their best bet at launching toys would be through a partnership with a company established in that industry. So, they presented their roster of characters to General Mills—the toy conglomerate that oversaw some of the world's most recognizable toy brands, including Kenner Toys. At that time, Bernie Loomis and his team had just finished launching the Star Wars line of toys, which remains one of the most successful launches to this day. Together, the folks from American Greetings and Bernie's team sifted through the collection of sketches until finally arriving at Strawberry Shortcake. The General Mills team fell instantly in love and decided that she would be the one they would run with.

This exchange is a perfect example of the foundation of licensing. It's a partnership between those who have the ideas and those who have the resources to turn those ideas into a major payday for all involved. This exchange is also how I wound up meeting my lifelong friend and colleague Carole MacGillvray, who was the vice president of marketing & design in the development division of General Mills under the auspices of the president, Bernie Loomis. This was the team that had recognized the opportunity to make Strawberry Shortcake a beloved children's character and wound up throwing their weight behind bringing her to the market. It was the late '70s, and Dobie was at the forefront of childrenswear manufacturing. I was the first person Carole and her team presented Strawberry Shortcake to, as they were looking to launch a line of Strawberry Shortcake apparel for kids.

Outside of being a marriage between people with ideas and people with the means to make these ideas a success, licensing is also a fancy way of describing how different companies piggyback on the efforts of others' brilliance. In order to introduce Strawberry Shortcake to the market, the team at General Mills was executing a brand-new strategy for getting mass attention. Their plan was to work with a production company to create a one-hour television special featuring Strawberry Shortcake that would air on Easter. They were coordinating with retailers to have products on shelves immediately after the program aired, to strike while the iron was hot and use the momentum of the anticipated success of the program to spark a frenzy of interest, causing products to fly off the shelves.

Being the licensee, I was not only interested in Strawberry Shortcake because I genuinely believed that she was an adorable character children and parents would love; I was also impressed with the amount of money and effort that the General Mills folks were putting into the marketing of this doll. The great thing about the licensing business is that everyone involved works alongside one another to support the common goal of a successful product launch. This allowed my team to stick to what we were good at: designing and manufacturing clothing that was original, functional, and durable. Everything we did had to be different; I'm quite certain that we even tried to make this clothing *smell* like the signature scent of the actual dolls.

Strawberry Shortcake's marketing strategy was planned down to every last detail, and General Mills was throwing millions of dollars into various campaigns as well as the Easter television special. Advertising is the backbone of any retail business, and in this case, a major national campaign was already underway. It was now up to our design team at Dobie to weigh in with our expertise in manufacturing and merchandising, and most importantly create high quality clothing that would help make the launch of Strawberry Shortcake a success.

This experience was an exciting one, and I was inspired by how big an impact our efforts had on the childrenswear market. The chance to join forces with this group of leaders that were working together to introduce Strawberry Shortcake was a great opportunity for Dobie to showcase what we did best, and way too impressive

158

to pass up. I was grateful that Carole and her team had approached me first, and I didn't hesitate to sign on the dotted line and become a part of the team behind one of the most recognizable children's characters in history. Strawberry Shortcake not only pioneered the concept of using movies and television to sell products to children, it introduced me to the opportunities licensing could bring and set the course of my career for years to come.

It's safe to assume that the vast majority of what's on retail shelves these days is a result of some sort of licensing agreement. To put it simply, licensing is a way of doing business that allows you to piggyback on the momentum of an idea or brand and explode it into a multifaceted revenue generator. Because of the reputation Dobie maintained as a credible and thoughtful clothing manufacturer, we continued to attract licensing opportunities from some of the industry's most creative minds who wanted us to play a role in taking their idea from unknown to undeniable. We worked with businesses from a wide range of industries—including books, sports, movies, television shows, events, and toys, to name a few. We were also plugged into a network of major retailers who trusted us enough to carry our lines. These retail stores often bought licenses themselves and created a team of people to support the introduction of certain characters to the market, and they thought enough of Dobie to allow us to produce merchandise for them under their license. Memorably, Sears Roebuck called us to produce part of their line of Winnie the Pooh, and J.C. Penney did the same thing once they secured the license for Sesame Street merchandise.

My approach to this industry was simple: Stay focused on pleasing the customer instead of working tirelessly to beat your competition, and everything else will fall into place. At the end of the day, all I ever tried to do was to take a simple shirt and make the front, back, and two sleeves as interesting as possible. The rest was a mixture of luck, opportunity, and integrity.

As I've mentioned, I did have my share of bad calls, including the Teenage Mutant Ninja Turtles and The Little Mermaid.

There was also the matter of a character not rendering correctly on a piece of clothing. And given that the originators of each design had first right of refusal, there was always a chance that our efforts could implode if the clothing didn't look good.

I was trying to bring the Where's Waldo character to life through a line of childrenswear. I thought that it would be a hit for sure, seeing as the books were captivating audiences all over Europe and North America. I flew out to London to meet with the creators of Where's Waldo, and they granted me the license to put him on our garments. I was excited, and thought I had Dobie's next hit on my hands. The challenge with the Waldo character was in the intricacy of the art and the tiny details of the sprawling scenes in which an almost invisible Waldo needed to be discovered. Unfortunately, the images never rendered properly on garments—perhaps because we were using knitted fabric—and the Where's Waldo folks rejected our samples and never gave us the final green light.

Many important factors go into a successful retail line, and it was our job to figure out ways to stay exciting, fresh, and creative in order to attract and keep customers. Since the early years of Dobie Originals and throughout my career, I made a point of hiring and surrounding myself with smart people who knew what they were doing. I was at least self-aware enough to realize that I didn't know everything about running a business—far from it—and with that in mind, I built a team of people who did. Back in the early '70s, I used to walk into different stores and go crazy as I noticed that matching tops and bottoms weren't displayed together, especially given the effort we made to perfectly match tops and bottoms. We created a matching system that sold our garments in matching sets according to coordinating colors, which was intended to solve the challenges of retail displays in the average department store. We named it Simple Systems, and the whole concept was to simplify shopping for parents by offering children's separates of coordinated tops and bottoms. It was also a huge win for us because it simplified the way the public received our merchandise while increasing the amount of merchandise on display. A big regret was never patenting the Simple Systems concept, as it wasn't long before our competitors implemented similar approaches.

The crux of my industry—if not most industries—was taking something so basic and making it exciting. My team and I also came up with the concept of Superwear, a line of clothing that was guaranteed to withstand two thousand washings, or customers would receive a refund. Since we already used high quality textiles to make durable apparel, all we had to do was highlight what we were doing. We simply added a money-back guarantee, and included a new label on each garment that clearly listed all of its inherently strong and durable characteristics. Customers loved the concept and the idea of a guarantee.

By the mid-1980s, I had come a long way from the tiny room I had rented in the back of a contractor's office to become the group executive of a large division of Cluett, Peabody Inc., which at the time was grossing over $1 billion dollars a year. I oversaw a collection of brands that included Dobie, Donmoore, Lady Arrow,

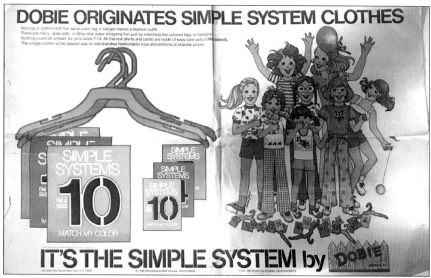

The Simple Systems idea was geared toward the mother who wasn't a designer. They could just come into the store and match a top to a bottom very easily.

Ron Chereskin, and Six Continents, and was truly in my element with a wonderful team of people. The network of buyers, department stores, and chain retailers had grown to trust me, and amidst all of my personal hardships, work had become my sanctuary, and the place in which I thrived. These were exciting and challenging times, and I felt grateful to be a part of this milieu.

During the mid-1980s, leveraged buyouts were a trend in business, thanks to heavyweight financiers like Michael Milken, who were able to raise large sums of money and raid their way through various industries, executing hostile takeovers on companies by acquiring the majority of their stock and then assuming the reins. Cluett, Peabody was a natural target for takeover artists because of the quality of our brands and the beauty of our balance sheet. But our board was strong, and management never once thought that we were at risk of being raided. That was until a young corporate raider named Paul Bilzerian set his sights on Cluett, and with the help of Michael Milken, he began stockpiling shares in an effort to obtain the majority of the company and ultimately take it over. Everyone in the company became concerned as Bilzerian continued to accumulate well over half of the company's shares, positioning him as the majority stakeholder.

For an established company proudly founded on a passion for creating trusted quality clothing for decades, this pending hostile takeover of the company was devastating. Cluett, Peabody was so highly respected, that to this day, it is named in a historical American clothing exhibit at the Smithsonian. Mr. Cluett and Mr. Peabody were pioneers of the men's shirt industry, going back to the cowboy days, when they developed that Western-style cuff and collar. The biggest concern during this was that Bilzerian's motives

163

were strictly financial, and the company wouldn't remain as stable and successful without the foundation of passion it was built on.

Luckily for us, a white knight rolled in and saved us from the pending hostile takeover of Cluett. Textile and home goods giant WestPoint Pepperell bought Bilzerian out at the beginning of 1986 and acquired Cluett, Peabody in a deal that most of us close to the company would say saved us. Several years later, Bilzerian fell into hot water with the Securities and Exchange Commission—this country's most intimidating financial regulator.

My colleagues and I were grateful to WestPoint for saving our group of companies from uncertainty. We all saw it as a great partnership, given that we both sold goods to the public. Life at Cluett changed nearly overnight. As the new company formed, it was a top priority to change some of the methods of doing business. Shortly after, we lost access to the company jet and gave up our company cars, and some of the extras that WestPoint at the time didn't view as necessities at the time. I was far from devastated, however, as my professional satisfaction came from much more than the luxuries and excess. I was just glad WestPoint saved us from Bilzerian's raid, and it was able to keep Dobie and Cluett, Peabody going, if not forever, for *just one more season!*

Joe Linear, CEO of WestPoint Pepperell, and my boss at Cluett, could have been cast in any Western movie. He was quintessential Southern charm in the form of a big business executive, and he had a wonderful presence, a great sense of humor, and was a pleasure to work with.

A few years after Bilzerian tried to raid Cluett and WestPoint swooped in to save us and buy him out, retail giant William Farley set his sights on us, and we were once again facing a raid. Farley was the CEO and chairman of Farley Inc., which was the holding company that owned and operated Fruit of the Loom, among other brands. Farley was a former banker turned takeover specialist who experienced formidable success throughout the 1970s through a slew of well-executed leveraged buyouts. He and his partners acquired Fruit of the Loom through the purchase of retail conglomerate Northwest Industries Inc., and together they built the brand into one of the most successful underwear companies of all time.

In late 1989, Farley and his team initiated efforts for a takeover of WestPoint, Cluett, and all of its subsidiaries—including mine. It was a complex deal in which Farley managed to acquire the vast majority of the stock and an ownership position for himself. He was determined to acquire the company and was willing to pay a high premium. On a personal level, this was great for me since I was able to sell off my shares at a favorable rate. But when all was said and done, this raid created a massive amount of debt because of the purchase price, and wound up knocking the company on its back. This ultimately put Cluett, Peabody in a position to declare bankruptcy, and the newly merged conglomerate soon began to collapse.

The whole ordeal was fascinating to me, and never in a million years would I have thought that I would be a part of the nucleus around which billions of dollars were exchanging hands. I was surrounded by captains of industry who were, at this time, fighting for their positions, and the familiar feeling of an uncertain future began to wash over me. The organization finally succumbed to its debtors and began selling off divisions and dissolving the company. It became astonishingly evident that the debt that the company assumed would be difficult to meet, especially if we were to run into tough times on the retail side.

For a brief moment, I considered what I would do if I lost everything and had to start over. Dobie itself had come a long way from its humble beginnings in a small office. Nat and I had built this company literally from the ground up, and I was prepared to do it again if I had to—although I dreaded the concept of being knocked so far backwards after spending decades working my way up to the position I was in. The uncertainty was paralyzing, and worry grew as I watched my parent company encounter financial difficulties. Consequently, they began to liquidate assets, and the company started to split up completely. Arrow shirts was sold to a company in France, and Gold Toe hosiery was acquired by a local manufacturer. The future of Dobie was unclear, but I assumed that it would be sold off just like the rest of our properties.

I felt like I was strapped into the last car of a roller coaster ride without a clue of what was to come next, only the knowledge that the movements were likely to be sharp and perhaps even terrifying. Farley and his team of advisors were rapidly selling off Cluett, Peabody properties in hopes of settling the overwhelming debt we had assumed during the takeover.

I felt like I was treading water amidst all the other executives, who were voicing concerns over facing what could perhaps be very strong decisions and changes. And then, in true form to the pattern of my life, luck struck, and I was offered the chance to buy back Dobie and assume full control. Cluett was selling off all of their properties, companies were being sold off, and because of the respect they had for us and the way Dobie operated, they gave me a very favorable deal to buy it back. Cluett's shareholders and top executives felt safer with me at the helm as opposed to the thought of some other company coming in to buy it.

Farley and their group and I reached a price that was acceptable to all parties involved, and we began to arrange a deal to buy the company back. The deal was based on a line of credit and valued at a favorable price, but the catch was that they also wanted me to personally guarantee the debt. This meant that if Dobie didn't perform well, I would essentially bridge the gap and pay down the debt out of my own pocket. I had no intention of doing this after a lifetime of building my assets and proving my salt as an executive.

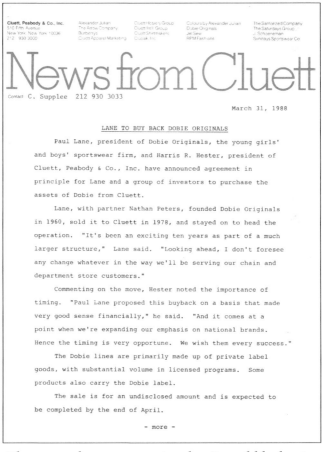

The press release announcing that I would be buying Dobie Originals back from Cluett.

I remember the day I was sitting in the offices of Chemical Bank with the executives in charge of the CIT Group, who lent money to people in situations like mine. They were doing their best to try and get me to personally guarantee the debt would be paid off from my pocket should the company underperform. I vehemently rejected every attempt and had no intention of budging on the idea.

"Come on, Paul, you know you can pull these numbers!" one of the bankers pleaded, working overtime to convince me to sign the guarantee. "The personal guarantee is just a formality so that the bank feels good about letting you assume this monstrous debt."

With a smile on my face, I shook my head in order to convey a firm "No, thank you." I had the money, but I was damn sure not going to dip into my own pockets to cover corporate debt caused by a few bad calls and a disaster of a merger. I also had a track record of integrity and promptly repaying any and all debts I took on to advance the business, and I firmly believed that there was no need for me to personally guarantee the debt.

This particular banking group had a long and close relationship with Dobie and me. After a lengthy back and forth, the bankers realized that they could feel confident with the terms of the loan and finally approved it. Regardless of the forthcoming roller coaster ride that would be the final chapter of my career, I did manage to settle this debt and pay the bank back in full.

So here we were in 1988, I was just about fifty-seven years old, and I had Dobie back completely in my hands. Nat and I continued on with business as usual, and I was ecstatic to once again be at the helm of the company I had started decades prior. I knew I was heading confidently toward a comfortable retirement, but I had no idea at the time that these final chapters would be the most tumultuous of my career in the clothing manufacturing business.

Chapter 14

Begin Again

AFTER FOURTEEN YEARS AS EXECUTIVES AT A LARGE public company, Nat and I were about to regain full control of the company we had started nearly twenty-five years earlier. By now, it was 1989 and I was back doing what I did best. It didn't feel like starting over, but rather a return to the role I was most comfortable in. During the Cluett era, I oversaw four companies as well as Dobie, and while each company was run by its own team of capable executives, they ultimately reported to me, and I was responsible for the overall operations of all of them.

Here we go again, I thought, excited about the fact that we had reclaimed Dobie for ourselves and could get back to marketing, merchandising, and manufacturing childrenswear. By this time, Dobie had evolved into an established company, which enabled us to hit the ground running once the ink on our buyback deal had dried. We still had many of the people from my original management group with us, which offered a sense of comfort, camaraderie, and familiarity. Much of Dobie's success could be attributed to how well this group worked together, and we were grateful to have a great team of executives who walked through the fire with us in Dobie's early years and then saw it all the way through to the buyback. Everyone on the team was excited about Dobie becoming a standalone company again, and the energy around the office was high. It truly felt like we were poised to experience the best years the company had ever seen.

As we began ramping up Dobie's operations in our office located at 1333 Broadway, it became apparent that there was a major paradigm shift occurring in the clothing manufacturing and retail industry, and the changes were happening rapidly. Large retail chains were swallowing up the smaller ones which, for us, meant a depletion in our roster of clients. After all, fewer chains meant fewer accounts to call on. And as the major retailers grew into conglomerates, their operations got bigger. And these big retailers were bringing production in-house and ultimately creating their own manufacturing departments under their own labels, in an effort to cut costs related to outsourcing, trimming their supply chain in order to optimize revenue in as many places as possible. This included sourcing licensing opportunities and working with our sources to keep the manufacturing of their goods in-house and ultimately increase their profit margins and bottom line.

This trend inevitably created challenges for us since some retailers no longer required the services of apparel manufacturers like us, and the ones who did began making demands that were previously unheard of. Retailers now expected the manufacturer's guarantee of certain returns on the merchandise sales with a refund attached if the goods didn't perform as well as we projected. They also began requesting that we as manufacturers facilitate the liquidation of unsold goods via other outlets at our expense.

This changed my view of the industry, as well as how we operated. Thankfully this didn't feel too threatening as Dobie had already established itself as a solid company. We would simply have to work harder and get a little creative to remain afloat in an industry that was rapidly evolving.

If I had one piece of advice to any entrepreneur out there, it would be that your integrity always determines your success. How you treat the people you work for or alongside at every level and whether you deliver on your promises are ultimately the determining factors of your success and professional longevity. This may seem like simple and obvious advice; however, I have watched many people crumble and lose their professional momentum because they traded in their integrity for short-term gratifications and seemingly insignificant victories. Everyone at Dobie was committed to maintaining our reputation, and it showed in the long-term relationships we had with so many of the different chains, department stores, and mail-order retailers we worked with. As companies were being pushed out because of the industry shifts that were taking place, we stayed strong and were able to keep going and to acquire major licenses and manufacture childrenswear as we had done for years.

Trust is also a major consideration in the world of licensing; the licensor had to trust that the licensee would ensure the art was great, the clothing was made well, and that they would receive their licensing check on the tenth of each month with no need to embark on any forensic accounting to confirm the numbers. Dobie was positioned as a trusted childrenswear manufacturer, which helped us to secure the licenses for some of the biggest and most well-known characters from film and television. After Nat and I regained full control of our company, we continued to pursue opportunities to license major characters to include in our apparel designs. These efforts continued to bring us out to Hollywood to vie for the rights of the iconic characters of the day.

It was a well-known fact that Spielberg was a great admirer of Walt Disney, and loved animation. This was rumored to be the catalyst of his partnership with Warner Brothers, which led to the creation of Tiny Toons in 1991. The idea for Tiny Toons was the brainchild of Dan Romanelli, who was the head of licensing for Warner Brothers at the time. He believed that this would not only be a formidable partnership between two industry heavyweights, but also a great way for Spielberg and his team to get involved with animation. This children's cartoon program was a spin-off of the world-famous Looney Toons show, and would feature a roster of young, whimsical characters who were written as the children of the original Looney Toons favorites. When two powerful forces like Amblin and Warner Brothers got together, the result was sure to be a hit. It quickly became evident that this project had all the makings of a major licensing opportunity: there were big names behind it, a TV show was rolling out, the characters were actually very cute, and licensees from other industries were on board with the show, developing toys and other product lines of their own that would feature the Tiny Toons characters.

We worked hard to obtain this license and managed to negotiate an exclusive deal from the Amblin and Warner Brothers companies, positioning Dobie as the sole manufacturer of Tiny Toons childrenswear.

Since it was not unusual for such a big license to be split amongst manufacturers in the same industry, I laid down a lot of money to be sure that I was the exclusive licensee for all of Tiny Toons' childrenswear. I was so sure this line was going to be a major hit that I would have laid down my entire savings just to secure it. The chairman of Warner Brothers himself had to personally sign the deal granting me this exclusivity, which, thankfully, he agreed to. We were on our way.

We were very confident that this line would take off the same way some of our previous lines had, and got right to work on product design and developing marketing and launch strategies. Because of Dobie's solid relationship with J.C. Penney, and considering their magnitude and size, they were the first retailer we approached with our Tiny Toons line.

When I traveled to Texas to meet with J.C. Penney's executives, I brought my friend Brad Globe, a good friend of Dan's who ran all of Spielberg's licensing. Brad was a natural when it came to licensing deals; he was talented and thoughtful in his approach and had a track record of successful deals, making him my first choice as far as pitch partners were concerned. Brad was able to help me present all the elements of the forthcoming line in a compelling and effective way, and the meeting with J.C. Penney was ultimately a success. After this meeting, Brad and I went out for brunch, and one of the most beautiful women I've ever seen in real life walked by our table and sat nearby. Brad couldn't help but admire her ... she certainly was a showstopper!

As I noticed my friend looking at her with admiration, I began prodding and teasing him as he squirmed in his seat, exuding shyness and humility. Brad was always the consummate gentleman.

I thought the world of Brad and was always one to look out for my friends. So, without skipping a beat, I got up and approached her and another woman who I assumed was her chaperone, and invited them both out for drinks at the end of the workday at the lobby bar of the hotel we all happened to be staying at. As it turned out, she was a model who was in town for a shoot, and the woman with her was, in fact, her chaperone. They obliged, and we all met up for an interesting evening of cocktails and pleasantries. I talked the chaperone into joining me in leaving these two alone since things seemed to be going smoothly. She agreed, and we both excused ourselves so Brad and the young lady could get to know each other a little better. I wished them well and headed off to catch my flight back to New York. When I landed, I received a call at about 3:00 a.m. from Brad saying that they had skipped town together and he was currently in the quaint town of Lubbock, Texas, continuing the conversation they had started at the hotel bar. I am quite certain he was calling me from a hot tub.

Brad and I have shared a formidable professional relation-ship and a friendship for nearly three decades. And while Brad's encounter with the model from Texas was merely a tryst, it was also a romantic testament to the fact that intense professional settings can bring unexpected surprises and ultimately, sometimes work can have its advantages.

Tiny Toon Adventures wound up becoming the number-one rated program for kids immediately following its inaugural broadcast, and stayed in that position for many years. Looking back at the launch of Tiny Toons, I do think that we would have been far more successful had we waited to launch the clothing, so the market could warm up to the program. TV programs are different than the movies. They have a longer lifespan and less of a marketing blitz surrounding their launch. As a general rule, licensees are much better served by holding back on the rollout of the merchandise related to TV programs and characters. When it comes to licensed goods, the timing of the launch will make or break their success. With this venture, we learned more lessons about the precision of licensing and the timing of its elements.

We continued to run the business the best way we knew how, with our eyes and ears peeled for opportunities to bring characters to life on our lines of childrenswear. Historically, Dobie had specialized in creating little girls' clothing. However, we were considering launching a line of boy's clothing with some of the characters from major action-adventure movies coming out of Hollywood. Dobie was able to secure the license to the infamous *Dick Tracy* movie directed by Warren Beatty. I had the pleasure of being invited to the set as the movie was being made, and was fascinated by how they were able to bring so much life into the animated characters. I also got to watch Madonna, Dick Van Dyke, and Warren Beatty himself in action. In spite of the fact that *Dick Tracy* was an adult-oriented film, I figured that the vast momentum behind the movie would spark an interest in kids who would then request their parents buy our clothing for them. We launched the line alongside the launch of the movie, but the merchandise didn't perform as well as some of the previous lines we had that featured kid-friendly characters. However, we would still continue to pursue major-motion-picture deals under the assumption that the sheer magnitude of the film would create a need for themed childrenswear that featured the main characters.

I flew out to the UK to visit the set of *Robin Hood*, in hopes of acquiring the license to render some of the characters from this movie on childrenswear. Kevin Costner was the star, many other companies were becoming licensees for the movie's merchandise, and I thought that such a big name would create a need in the market for childrenswear. It was obvious that these movies skewed older, but there was such a powerful backing behind the product that I figured a line of childrenswear would be very effective. Much like our *Dick Tracy* line, the *Robin Hood* apparel ended up performing adequately, but nothing like the magnitude of the previous lines we did that had an obvious and overt focus on younger children.

I began to realize that we needed to revert to finding licenses for characters that were obviously for young children. We were constantly on the hunt for our next Strawberry Shortcake or Care Bears.

During one of my many regular conversations with Henry Scott, the president of J.C. Penney, he began regaling me with tales about this purple dinosaur who was creating pandemonium in a small town near Dallas. His grandson could not stop raving about this homegrown character named Barney—a big purple dinosaur with a big heart and an unforgettable song to sing.

I was intrigued to say the least. When someone like Henry Scott speaks up with an idea, it's generally a good plan to listen. I knew he had great instincts for marketing and merchandising. Out of sheer curiosity, I ended up flying down to a small town close to Dallas, where Barney fever had the local children hypnotized. There, I found myself in the stands of a high school football stadium packed to the gills with children screaming and cheering as a convertible pulled onto the field, with Barney waving and cheering from the back. The volume of screams and cheers increased, and all at once the audience quickly dove into their rendition of the now-famous signature song, "I Love You, (You Love Me." I knew instantly that this had great potential, and I was ready to sink my teeth right into it.

I was overwhelmed by the response the kids in the audience had to Barney. Their excitement compelled me to seek out the company that was producing Barney as well as Barney's creator, Sheryl Leach. She was a former school teacher who initially created Barney as a learning aid for her classroom, but had left her job by the time I met her to devote her time to developing the Barney character, with the support and encouragement of her family. From the moment I met her, I knew she was someone special. Sheryl felt comfortable enough with me to share the fact that she is an avid meditator, and this goofy purple dinosaur appeared in a vision during one of her meditations. I was on my own path to wellness and absolutely believed in the power of meditation as a powerful tool for relaxation and uncovering ideas lying dormant in various corners of the mind.

By this time, Sheryl had teamed up with a production studio to create children's videos titled *Barney and the Backyard Gang* and other content that would continue to support the development of Barney as a teaching tool. The content was performing as well as a collection of children's VHS tapes could, but Sheryl and her team knew that they had created a hit, and at that time were looking to bring Barney to a bigger network.

One day in 1991, the daughter of a Connecticut Public Television executive rented the video and was in a frenzy of admiration for Barney. Her dad had the same instinctual reaction that I did, realizing that it could be perfect to pitch to PBS. He shared the video with a few of his network colleagues, and they all returned with the same feedback: their kids absolutely loved Barney. PBS funded the production and ran it on their affiliate stations for thirty days as a trial period.

In spite of the show being a smash success, PBS decided not to extend funding after the thirty-day period had ended. Upon hearing this news, some of the affiliates wrote letters to PBS executives, urging them to reconsider their decision to pull the plug on this obviously beloved children's character. They also sent out messages to the Barney Fan Club, urging parents of fans to write letters or call in to their local PBS station to show support for the Barney show. By the time the annual PBS affiliates meeting rolled around that year, PBS changed its mind and extended funding for the *Barney & Friends* show indefinitely.

After seeing the organic love for this goofy creature and seeing all the work being done by a wonderful team of creatives to promote Barney, I began to pursue the license, confident that it had all the potential required to become a smash success in the world of childrenswear. I positioned the idea to the team behind Barney as a chance to expand the brand and develop undeniable traction from Barney's loyal fans. Sheryl agreed, and saw it as another way to increase awareness of her beloved character, and gave Dobie the exclusive license to manufacture the Barney childrenswear. The Barney frenzy continued to grow worldwide, and by the time our line hit the shelves, parents and kids were salivating over the merchandise. It was like watching a storm develop without having any idea of its eventual magnitude.

The world became utterly mesmerized by Barney. Everyone around me asked if I knew him or had ever met him, to which I replied that he was kept hidden in order to keep up the façade. It was fun to keep up the fairy tale to the Barney lovers as I watched Dobie's merchandise fly off the retail shelves. We all knew early that Barney was a big hit, and calls from merchandisers ordering more Barney clothes kept coming in.

We did it! I thought. *We found our next Strawberry Shortcake.* Children and parents all over the world were hypnotized by this purple dinosaur, and Dobie helped them display their love for the character via their wardrobe. Our art department worked vigorously to create new and inventive ways to render Barney and his friends on children's clothing, and it seemed like everything Barney touched turned to gold.

A few nights ago, I was having dinner at my club with a few friends when one of the hostesses approached my table to thank me for my contribution to her life—which turned out to be in the form of Barney the Dinosaur. She couldn't have been more than thirty years old. Someone must have pointed me out as being part of the team of people that had brought Barney to the mainstream, and she felt compelled to share with me the impact it made on her life. It got me thinking about my career as a merchant, and everything that went into the process of licensing. If done correctly, the practice of licensing can take a relatively simple idea and explode it into a phenomenon that clearly has the potential to create a lasting impression. I've traveled the world and shared many of my life's stories, but I continue to receive the biggest reaction when I talk about that goofy dinosaur with a song that nobody can ever seem to get out of their head.

Chapter 15

Walking Away

IT WAS NOW 1992, AND THE PRESIDENTIAL RACE WAS taking place between Bill Clinton, George Bush, and Ross Perot. The scope of American labor had shifted, and many workers were jumping ship and abandoning the apparel manufacturing world to join the tech industry. Because of this, staffing manufacturing facilities started to become more and more of a challenge. At the same time, Mexican companies were looking for opportunities to invest in American companies and establish a corporate presence in the US, which wound up setting the stage for the North American Free Trade Agreement (NAFTA) between the United States, Canada, and Mexico. NAFTA was the hot-button issue of that year's US presidential election, designed to promote commerce and fair trade between the United States, Canada, and Mexico; however, it garnered very mixed opinions.

Ross Perot was loudly and vehemently against this trade agreement, and felt like companies sending their labor to Mexico meant yanking jobs and opportunities from the American worker. He wasn't wrong, but he was failing to consider that there was a labor shift in the US workforce that was causing the labor employment force to migrate over to the technology sector. It was fairly straightforward: the tech industry paid more than the apparel manufacturing industry did, and the labor force was adjusting their skills and vocation accordingly. Dobie and countless other clothing manufacturers were affected by the shift, and it led us to start shopping for labor options outside of America.

Mexico seemed to be a natural choice because of its proximity to the US and how far our dollar was able to stretch in that country and work in that field. Because of the global strength of the American dollar at the time, labor costs in Mexico were cheaper than the wages we paid in the United States, which substantiated these types of commercial partnerships even further.

Now, what did this have to do with Dobie?

At the same time NAFTA was ramping up, a group of successful local Mexican executives teamed up with an American venture capitalist and set their sights on buying companies in America, and Dobie was one of the companies they pursued. Our children's line was thriving, and our recently launched ladies' line was well on its way to becoming a success. The deal was seen as being mutually beneficial, as the Mexican investors saw it as an opportunity to participate in American commerce, and Dobie would have the opportunity to strengthen and expand our manufacturing operations in Mexican factories. The deal was being put together and was in the process of being signed and somehow, Ross Perot caught wind of it. He called it out on TV as an example of a company that was selling out to Mexico. It was frightening and shocking at the same time—to think my movements had caught the eye of a presidential hopeful! Ultimately, while he was against the notion of moving jobs from America to Mexico, he failed to understand that we no longer had a deep pool of manufacturing workers in America and needed the opportunity to hire Mexican workers in order to keep Dobie thriving.

The deal moved forward, and the Mexican firm was preparing to buy Dobie in a similar deal that Cluett had struck: our leadership and management teams would remain the same, while our labor force would ultimately be strengthened by Mexican manufacturing facilities. After many, *many* meetings and rounds of due diligence, the deal was nearly done. And all the while Barney was continuing to skyrocket, becoming one of the world's most beloved and recognizable children's characters. During this time, Joe Linear, CEO of WestPoint Pepperell and my former boss at Cluett, jokingly accused me of snookering him during negotiations for me to buy back Dobie. Given the success the company was experiencing through Tiny Toons, Barney, and the other lines, perhaps he felt like I was holding back until I regained the company, and he was privy to Dobie's financial information since he held the debt acquired through the buyback. I quickly explained that having my time freed up from constant meetings meant I was able to focus solely on Dobie, which changed everything. Time and focus allowed me to go full steam ahead in terms of Dobie's goals and objectives, and Barney was just one of the reasons why this company was thriving. Joe ultimately understood and accepted my explanation and wished me luck.

In my role, I often felt like a movie producer since our projects were always major productions with many moving parts. The clothing manufacturing industry faced four seasons: winter, spring, summer, and the holidays; Christmas accounted for a large part of our sales. Another noticeable shift in my industry was the fact that children had much more of a say in the clothing their parents purchased for them than they did back in my earlier days. Interestingly, these kids were steadily becoming more and more interested in what they were wearing, and it showed in the decisions they were making. The designers and I spent more time than usual visiting stores all over the US, Europe, and Montreal to see what was selling. We always tried to stay on the cutting edge of children's fashion, and we were able to thrive in spite of the industry growing tougher and more competitive as time went on. We made it our job to consider what was trending in high fashion and incorporate those styles into our lines at an affordable price.

This merger deal was coming to a close, and the Mexican firm seemed excited about how Dobie was performing. I was invited down to Mexico to meet with the investors and was overwhelmed by the graciousness and hospitality I received while I was there. It was quite a revelation for me to see the lifestyle of successful Mexican entrepreneurs. I went to individual homes that were the size of cities, with custom-built private bullrings, and witnessed wealth and prosperity in ways I'd never seen before. They were a group of insightful and enterprising businessmen who seemed to share quite a kinship with Dobie, and we ended up signing a deal for them to acquire us.

As you may recall from a previous chapter, I had become quite the boating enthusiast during these years. Shortly after the Mexican investors acquired Dobie, I was gearing up to return in my boat from Nantucket to Montauk. We were packed and ready to go, and as I reached down to untie the ropes from the dock and set sail, a stabbing pain radiated through my chest. While it was uncomfortable, I chalked it up to heartburn and set off on my journey up the East Coast. As I got close to the docks in Montauk, I once again reached down to tie up the boat and was greeted by the same sharp pain I was met with hours earlier. I knew heartburn shouldn't last this long, so I made an appointment with my cardiologist to be safe. The appointment was scheduled on the same day I was heading to San Francisco for a series of meetings. With my suitcase and retail samples in tow, I stopped in at the cardiologist's office. We exchanged pleasantries and I shared the details of the pain I experienced on the boat but emphasized the fact that I was certain it was nothing. And in a charismatic quest to prove that there was nothing for the doctor to be concerned about, I dropped down and gave twenty push-ups in the middle of the exam room. The doctor chuckled, and we began wrapping up the appointment.

"Just a minute, Mr. Lane," the doctor began, just as I was just about to leave his office. He explained to me that he would be remiss if he didn't perform one more test on me, in light of my recent experiences with chest pain. He attached several wires and monitors to my chest and instructed me to get on the treadmill. I obliged. However, a few short moments after beginning a light run, the doctor called for a wheelchair, and I was rushed to an operating room.

Turns out that my arteries were blocked, and I was on the fast track to my own death. The doctor performed an emergency angiogram—which is the injection of a special dye into the veins that can help doctors pinpoint blockages and other oddities. They were able to find where it was and open it up through a procedure that resembled drilling for oil. This moment was just months before the approval of heart stents—a medical tool that helps blood flow unhindered through the arteries, so they had to do it the old-school way. The doctors managed to successfully clear the artery and released me with a clean bill of health and resting orders and I was back at work a few days later.

My prompt return to work seemed to impress the new Mexican partners, and I received plenty of kudos for my dedication. In my mind, my speedy recovery was merely a testament to the excellent medical care I had been lucky enough to receive. Plus, my blood was flowing better than it had before I went in the hospital, and I was experiencing a youthful vitality that I had had no idea was missing. This health scare wound up being a rejuvenating force that I believe may have ultimately added years to my life.

The reception I received upon my relatively speedy return seemed to solidify the formidable relationship that had grown between me and our new Mexican partners. The American investor who was at the helm of this merger seemed enthusiastic about the impact Dobie was continuing to make on the childrenswear industry, and we were constantly conferring about new ideas and opportunities for Dobie as well as other companies he was interested in buying. I was focused on building the company, and our partnership with the Mexican investors felt like a whole new opportunity. I was thrilled with the way things were developing, and there was an obvious level of camaraderie between Dobie's team and the Mexican investors. I was, however, beginning to feel some discomfort with the banker because he was spending too much time around the premises talking to our people. Usually, the investors partake in their due diligence prior to any merger or acquisition and aren't as inquisitive after the fact. He was asking too many questions, to the point at which it seemed like he was snooping around.

Things seemed to be moving in a positive and lucrative direction, and Barney continued to explode all over the globe. Dobie remained in a constant state of growth and the future seemed bright for all of us. Not long after the merger was finalized, the Mexican group decided that it would be a great time to take Dobie public. At their behest, they began to seek out an underwriter to begin preparing all of the necessary steps to start the IPO. This was a delicate process with many moving parts and called for the presentation of a ton of information, including our current financial standing and our projections for the future. I joined them in interviewing potential underwriters, but in the end, the Mexican group made the final hiring decision. The underwriter began to gather the documents and projections necessary for a preliminary prospectus of the offering, also known as a red herring. As we moved through this process, everyone seemed happy and excited about going public. I agreed that the public offering would be a great way to solidify Dobie's longevity, and would put myself and some of the other executives and shareholders into a healthy financial position. It truly was an exciting time.

The company was all abuzz and moved full steam ahead with the preparation of the public offering and assembly of the red herring. One afternoon, an executive from the accounting firm we had worked with for decades was sitting in on one of our sales meetings and overheard some of the projections for the year. We were discussing some of the weaknesses in our sales patterns, and from this he deduced that the numbers projected in our red herring might be a little bit aggressive. He had been working with Dobie for long enough to have solid knowledge of our past patterns and a valid understanding of our performance history. It seemed to me like the accountant felt as if he had a fiduciary responsibility to share this information with the underwriter, who wound up agreeing with the accountant.

Word began to spread through the executive level of Dobie that there was some concern about our projections. While some of the management would have liked to forge ahead with the IPO, the underwriter made the final decision to temporarily hold up the process, at least until he had a better understanding of our company and was able to update the numbers to reflect more attainable projections. Personally, I remained enthusiastic about taking Dobie public and was hell-bent on doing so, but only if the numbers were appropriate and not too aggressive. So, on the advice of the underwriter, Dobie's IPO was temporarily halted.

News of the IPO's delay spread, and there was a collective feeling of disappointment. The Mexicans didn't necessarily agree with the underwriter's assessment, and the American investor who orchestrated the entire acquisition was furious over the news of the delay. He wound up directing his fury toward me and made it clear that he felt I was sabotaging the underwriting. Considering what I stood to gain from Dobie going public, this assumption was far from accurate and made absolutely no sense.

I was taken aback by this hostility and couldn't figure out why he wasn't on the same page as I was. I could understand why he was disappointed, but I was curious about why he was so angry. It wasn't over; this was merely a delay. But in hindsight, it seemed as if this man was more concerned about what he reported back to his shareholders than running a solid, quality business. The tension continued. As colleagues, we were cordial to each other and he shared some of what he considered to be business insights throughout our time together, but in hindsight, we never really got along on a personal level. Prior to this entire ordeal, we did butted heads from time to time. He had a certain way he wanted things done. He knew nothing about this industry, and I simply wasn't accustomed to someone meddling in Dobie's operations and questioning my judgment. I did feel that we may have been moving too fast and thought that a delay would have given us more time to prepare instead of seeming like we were trying to take the money and run.

Tensions continued to mount between us and sadly, a few of the key Mexican investors shared his view that we should have forged ahead with the IPO, looking to me as the reason why it all seemed to have fallen apart. The investor continued to rally some of the management team against me, and the tension and the atmosphere in our company became unpleasant, to say the least. This wasn't the way we did business at Dobie, neither on our own nor when we were with Cluett, Peabody. I finally mentioned that if everyone was so unhappy with me, perhaps I could just leave. Sadly, no one put up a fight, and within two days I walked away from Dobie for good. Some said what I did was stupid, and some said it was moral. Either way, I was done.

The first few days after I left were quite painful; I never wanted to leave this way. The announcement was made, and shock rippled through the company as word spread that I was out. In the wake of the announcement, my colleagues slapped together a last-minute party to thank me before I left. There were so many people in the company who had worked for Dobie since the beginning of their careers, so this was truly a gathering of folks I had grown to care deeply about over the years. The news of my departure came as a shock to everyone, and there were many tears, hugs, and thank-yous. However, given everything that had occurred, coupled with the major shifts that were taking place all over my industry, I was ready to go. Admittedly, I was very sad about the idea of leaving the people I had spent so many years building the company with. But the truth was I just wasn't excited about what I was doing anymore. Ultimately, I had come to terms with the fact that this era of my life had come to an end, and I felt that this was a good time to go.

One of the biggest disappointments of this whole ordeal was that my partner Nat didn't walk out alongside me. I wanted him to come with me in solidarity, but he ended up staying with the company, and our thirty-year friendship crumbled because of it. In my heart I am certain that he knew what I did was right, but the disappointment of not getting more money seemed to bring about strange behavior. Nat remained furious because he too lost a lot of money when Dobie's IPO was delayed.

In the wake of my departure, I heard through the grapevine that my successor was a young MBA who claimed to have the same connections and abilities as I did. From what I heard, this turned out not to be the case, and news began to spread that Dobie's future was becoming uncertain. About a year and a half after I walked away, Dobie closed its doors permanently. By that time, I was too long gone for this news to be devastating. It was like hearing any other news story.

So, there you have it—I went from sitting in the army barracks as a kid, afraid of what my future held, to building a career in an industry that I wound up falling in love with. I truly lived the

American Dream, and to this day I am still in awe of the series of events that brought me from a terrified young father to an exciting life as an executive in the apparel industry.

As abruptly as my career ended, I was intrigued by the idea of slowing down and experiencing life outside of the world of work. I was sixty-three years old and had been in the workforce for exactly fifty years. I shifted gears and began to focus on making up for the time I never had growing up, since I spent my free time working from the age of thirteen onward.

In retrospect, I recognized my jealousy that other kids didn't have to work as hard as I'd had to, and they grew up playing sports and going to the parties I wasn't able to attend because of my work schedule and our family's financial need. I had watched in envy as friends and classmates went off to college while I continued working and then got drafted into the army. To this day I feel pangs of jealousy whenever friends reminisce on their college days.

By the time I left Dobie, all of my biggest responsibilities had been taken care of and I had accomplished everything I'd set out to do. Each of my three kids was completely independent, with a life, career, and family of their own. After a lengthy battle with several illnesses, my mom passed away, and the weight of worrying about and caring for her had been lifted. And I had absolutely no interest in continuing my career, in spite of the influx of offers that came in once word spread that I was a free agent. I was completely done with board meetings, banks, accountants, retailers, and the daily fires I had faced and done my best to put out. I considered the retired era of my life I was about to embark on as payback for working hard. This newfound freedom was quite the aphrodisiac.

I was always concerned and curious before I retired. The stories

I'd heard about retirement ranged from people who loved it to people who were never able to unravel their identity from their career and were never able to feel fulfilled. I also heard it could be difficult to transition from an executive position to someone with a self-regulated schedule, as one left the office on Friday and arrived at breakfast in pajamas on Monday. One thing I was certain of was that if I began to crave structured productivity or got bored, there were other jobs I could look into and other things I could do. That turned out not to be the case; I have not been bored a day in my retirement. Not long into it, I realized that it should be approached just like a career, and the same instincts that helped me be successful in business would ultimately help me be successful in retirement. I was ready for the fun and frivolity that I was looking forward to experiencing in this next era of my life, but had no idea of the level of tragic loss on the horizon.

Chapter 16

A Letter from Rita

ON MARCH 2, 2018, MY LIFE WAS FOREVER ALTERED. It was the evening of my grandson's engagement party, which took place in a beautiful restaurant in downtown Manhattan. It was a joyous occasion shared by our friends and family, and everyone adored my grandson Jonathan and his fiancée, Lizzie. Cocktails were underway, and I was receiving congratulations from guests who were toasting the couple. Not long into the evening, my phone rang—it was my sister Sheila, so I stepped out to take it. She was in Florida at the time visiting our sister Rita, and I instantly had a feeling that something was up.

"Paul, Rita took a pretty bad fall," she explained from her end of the phone in Florida. "I'm here in the hospital with her. She's in a coma."

For a second, my vision blurred, and my heart stopped. I was just with Rita not too long before this, and she was in top form for an eighty-nine-year-old woman. I was in a hazy combination of confusion and disbelief but decided immediately that I must keep my composure and not deplete any joy from the evening whatsoever. I continued on with the celebrations, performing as a complete shell of a man, and about half an hour later, I received another call from Sheila:

"Paul, they're thinking about pulling the plug," Sheila managed to utter between sobs. "Doctors say that in the best-case scenario, she will come out of this a vegetable."

I couldn't catch my breath. Having the wind sledgehammered out of my chest while having to maintain composure and a face that didn't let anyone in on what was really going on drained every ounce of my energy. The shock-fueled adrenaline was probably the only thing keeping me on track. I continued to give the performance of a lifetime for the party guests while completely unsure of the fate of Rita, who to me was one of the most important people in the world and the longest, most impactful relationship I had in my life.

As the night went on, my anxiety peaked with concern, but I fought with everything I had to exude only excitement and pride for my grandson and family. I was holding myself together by a fraying thread, and I knew there was no way I'd be able to get to Florida until the next morning at the earliest. I continued to go through the motions of the evening with the heaviest heart and the biggest hope that my phone wouldn't ring again.

I was able to convince a whole room of people that I was just the grandfather of the groom-to-be, and not a man who was steadily unraveling at the uncertainty of the fate of his beloved sister. About an hour after Sheila's first call to me that night, I felt the familiar buzz coming from the pocket that contained my phone. My heart stopped as I pulled my phone out to see Sheila's name flash across the screen. I ran out of the restaurant for the third time.

"Yeah," I managed to choke out, far too paralyzed with fear to wrap my mouth around the word *'hello.'*

"She's gone," Sheila said.

It was as if every last drop of liquid had been drained from my body, and I was dust. In less than the time it takes to eat dinner, I lost the last remaining human connection to my childhood. Just like that, in the span of one engagement party, my perfectly healthy sister was taken from me. It was one of the most ridiculous nights of my life as devastation ripped through my insides, but I still managed to keep my exterior in order, and not a single soul was aware of the ordeal I was enduring. To this day, I shudder thinking of the pain I had to suppress, when all I wanted to do was scream, cry, and run far away from any sort of celebration.

In one fell swoop, my whole world had changed forever. I would never be the same after this loss of my mother figure, sister, and best friend. Rita had been my only contact to my childhood and the life I had before I was successful. I did and still do love my sister Sheila just as dearly, but we don't share the same lengthy history.

I began putting together these memories around six months after Rita passed away, and the memory lane this project has forced me down has been simultaneously wonderful and devastating. Looking through the boxes and books of old photos and memories only highlights the vast gap that Rita's death has left in my life. There is no way I could complete this book without honoring Rita as she deserves and sharing the impact she made on me and every life she touched throughout her time on earth.

Me with my loving sister.

One afternoon as I was going through old pictures and press clippings, looking for information to share in my book, I stumbled across a letter Rita had written me. I had forgotten all about it, but reading through it brought the magic of Rita back to life. While short, it is definitely the perfect representation of who she was and how she loved. The letter starts:

Dear Paul,

Believe it or not I always felt the scales were tipped in your favor. Brawn, brains, looks, height, charm, audacity, courage—you have it all. Deep inside where no one goes but me, I've always felt jealous of all your attributes and yet I feel a part of all those virtues are also a part of me ...

When I was a kid, the death of my father and my mother's perpetual indifference toward me, would have left me completely without a support system if it weren't for my sister Rita. We did bicker about the usual things a brother and sister would bicker about, but the death of my father solidified a bond between us, resulting in our lives being completely intertwined for nearly seventy-five years. Both of us were in shock over the loss of my father, who had seemed to be in perfect health all the way up to his final day, much like Rita. From that day on, we became a team, overcoming every obstacle that newfound poverty presented.

The letter continued:

... I am reflected in you as you are in me. I've experienced love and hate but always my love and respect for you outweighs anything else ...

My sister was revered by my mother and nearly everyone around us. Rita was protected and cared for as if she were a United States gold mine. I was just a chubby, pimply-faced kid who was overlooked by everyone except for Rita. She looked at me like I was Clark Gable, and the mark she left on me that remains present to this day is the knowledge that in spite of how little I may have had to offer—especially as a youngster—being loved made me feel like a million bucks. Rita had this effect on everyone though. She was able to make anyone feel like they were the most interesting and important person on the globe. This was the epitome of her presence.

I think of her as an angel. I've never seen anyone—from then till now—who possesses the traits that she had. Aside from being extraordinarily beautiful to the point that heads turned everywhere we went, she had a basic sense of sweetness and kindness and was absolutely magnetizing. She had many friends growing up and was always the nucleus of the group and the leader in all the activities she was a part of. Rita had an inherent gift for kindness, gentleness, and caring for anyone who crossed her path.

We've come such a long way and I guess I am feeling reflective at age fifty. I realize a major portion of my life is over. Now going back, I never really aspired to be much more than I am, other than a fantasy or two about a beautiful ballerina or a prima donna soprano …

At the age of twenty, Rita married a man who by all standards was considered wealthy. Her life was a far cry from the poverty we grew up in; she was now in the lap of luxury with cars, homes, vacations, and everything else that came along with her husband's wealth. But never once did it go to her head. Through it all, she was the same kind and loving person. The chubby kid I once was had turned into an awkward, fat teenager, but Rita was always there by my side, counseling me on all my problems, from friends to part-time jobs to girls. If I was heading out to a party, Rita would make me join her in the hallway so she could teach me steps to the cha-cha and the rumba. We were like Fred Astaire and his older sister, Adele, who spent close to their entire lives dancing together. I can remember the magical moments of what ended up being our last dance, at my granddaughter Jessica's wedding. They played a rumba for us, and we nailed every step.

With age came a deeper bond between Rita and me. We were truly a legendary brother-sister duo, and I never stopped looking up to her. Rita had a nurturing compassion about her and a loyalty to her loved ones that was unbreakable. She had three sons on her own whom she doted on endlessly, but still found the time and resources to look after our mother in such a way that she didn't need to work to earn a living. Rita was also the voice in my head that motivated me to make my mother a priority as well, in spite of how she'd ignored me for most of my life.

I'm aware that many things have been easy for me, perhaps that is why I lacked motivation to do many things that I would have liked to do but never did. I lacked your wonderful tenaciousness and determination to do instead of just talk.

Unfortunately, Rita's wondrous kindness did not shield her from the onslaught of devastation she would face in the later years of her life.

Rita and her husband, Marty, had three children and a daughter-in-law, whom Rita loved with her entire being. Rita's first tragedy was the loss of her husband, which, as I have said, she found out about while she was dropping me at the airport. I still wish this news was delivered differently—it was such an ugly way to be told such a thing. But here we were.

In the weeks and months following the Marty's passing, Rita really stepped up to the plate. She naturally assumed the role of head of household, taking care of her kids, the bills, and anything else Marty generally handled. It was extremely impressive that even in the face of such tragedy, Rita possessed the courage to go on. It became quite clear that this was a trait that ran in our family.

Her youngest son, Steven, died at fifty-four of a heart attack, and a short time after, her middle son Alan, a doctor, died from an aggressive form of kidney cancer that we did our best to fight but wound up losing to in the end.

Diane, the wife of Rita's eldest son Jason, was next on the list of tragedy. Diane was an impressive woman with a PhD in Literature, a beautiful smile, and a warmth that could melt an iceberg. She developed ovarian cancer and fought hard for her life, but ended up dying a few years ago. That loss was devastating to our family. Diane was more like a daughter to us, as she and Jason had been together since they were fifteen years old.

As if our family—especially Rita—had not been through enough, her oldest son Jason was diagnosed with another form of cancer. According to doctors, he should have died a few times, but thanks to modern technology and continuing treatment, he survived and has a bright future in front of him. He is currently winning his battle with bladder cancer, and his survival and his life are a testament to the skills of the medical profession. Rita was still alive when he received his diagnosis amidst the flurry of death and tragedy her family experienced. What Rita went through was overwhelming for our family; I've delivered far too many eulogies in my life.

After the tornado of devastation seemed to subside, and Rita was nearly completely alone, the family did what we had done throughout our whole lives: supported each other through tragedy and worked on focusing on the good memories instead of the devastation that comes with loss. Our lives were always intertwined with each other, and she also followed the New York to Florida route after her husband retired. She lived just thirty minutes from me in Florida, and we spent more time together during this time than we had growing up and as young adults. On the surface, Rita may have seemed like a different woman as a result of the insane losses she had endured over the years, but she still had that same sparkle in her eye that she'd always had, and I loved her for it.

Not too many regrets. I'm rambling on when I just wanted to say thank you for being my brother, for loving me, for loving my sons and my husband.

Your sister,

Rita

I've never considered myself special, but I do consider myself lucky for having had Rita as my sister. I remember seventy-five women threw my sister a surprise party, and I was the only man who was allowed to come. One by one, people would stand up and make speeches, and each one referred to Rita as their best friend. My children loved their Aunt Rita. I often think that her innate sweetness was the buffer between the kids and my overly ambitious disciplinarian technique. Whenever I was being tough or had to discipline them, they would run to her, and she would comfort them and then call to yell at me about being too hard on them.

All three of my wives were impacted by Rita. She stood by Joan and held her hand until she died. Rita was even accepting of my famously awful second marriage, and Iris adored her. And to this day, Brenda continues to miss her terribly and feels as if she lost a best friend.

The world's reaction to Rita's untimely passing was overwhelming. People came from all over to pay their respects. She truly was a friend to all, regardless of their economic or social status. I just keep thinking Rita has been reincarnated and is doing this all again in some other life, bringing out the best in her loved ones and making everyone around her feel special and loved.

When I think back, the greatest relationship I've had in life was with my sister. The hole that remains because of this loss is a crater. It's huge. I just bought a new car and was devastated when I realized that this would be the first time I wouldn't drive the car off the lot and right over to Rita's to play show-and-tell. She knew how much I loved cars and would always put on a show of enthusiasm and delight each time I got a new one.

Much like when Joan passed, our family put a lot of effort into keeping Rita's legacy of kindness and warmth alive. We wanted to honor her for what she brought to our lives at every phase, especially as I went from an awkward kid to a young husband to a father to a businessman.

My feelings these days are deep longing and gratitude for being lucky enough to have had Rita in my life for all those years. Ongoing tragedy has always been a permanent backdrop to a wonderful time. The eras of my life have each been full of success as well as relentless drama, and retirement has proved no different. Sometimes I feel like the last man standing, and once—and sometimes several times—per week, I will receive a call that another friend or loved one has passed on. I guess the truth is that my story doesn't have an inspiring ending because it's a true testament to the old saying that life is a journey, not a destination. Everybody's life becomes a story, and I believe that it is important to share stories in order to solidify your own legacy and help make those around you feel like they are less alone.

Chapter 17
Retirement & Insights

RETIREMENT IS A DIFFERENT EXPERIENCE FOR EVERY-
ONE. Many executives who had careers like mine approach
retirement with hesitation and fear, because so much of their
identity is associated to their work. A common fear of high-level
executives is the fear of retirement—you go from having your
name on the door of your office on Friday to your wife making
you breakfast at home the following Monday. And there isn't much
reason to change out of your pajamas. I however, tried to look at
this completely differently and considered my exit to be perfect
timing with a touch of disappointment over how it all went down,
but ultimately, I was glad I left when I did. I now felt completely
free. My children were self-sufficient and successful, and I was
embarking on an era which, by design, would be dedicated to doing
whatever I want.

If I wake up in the morning and am able to stretch my arms
without touching the inside of a coffin, I know everything else will
be okay for the day. In spite of five separate health battles that
could have each been fatal, I'm still here, and ironically, I am better

(and busier!) than ever. I've only just come to realize how grossly underpaid our secretaries were now that I have to do everything for myself. I'm in a constant state of awe when it comes to technology, and I can't even say that I am at all savvy with a computer. I can sell the hell out of a Strawberry Shortcake outfit but continue to struggle with the intricacies of attaching a document to an email.

One of the most interesting realizations of life also comes during these later years, although it is something that many of us have been anxious about for most of our adult lives. It's during this time that you learn that passion and romance are not exclusive to the youth. Quite the opposite, actually. With the help of jewelry and a few bouquets here and there, I can honestly say that there is still very much a spark between Brenda and me.

Shortly after the dust of my sudden departure from Dobie had settled, we took off for Europe and drove thousands of miles through France, Spain, and Italy, visiting some of the most beautiful places in the world. When I returned to New York, I would see executives in the elevators of my building carrying briefcases while I was wearing boating clothes … it was a bit embarrassing. My accountant wound up convincing me to sell my New York home and become a permanent resident at my home in Florida, if for nothing else but the weather and tax benefits.

My proudest moments of retirement involved proudly watching my own children and grandchildren excel in all that they do. My kids all recognized the importance of growth and independence in their lives, and they are all thriving as hard-working, creative, self-sufficient human beings. I am humbled to look at their lives and see that maybe, just maybe, they *were* influenced by me and the way I lived my life, both personally and professionally. The same can be said for my grandkids. I live a very proud man, but it wasn't always the most liberating and fun period of my life. As you've read by now, my later years became riddled with more tragedy, as I watched how sickness ravaged and destroyed my sister Rita's entire family.

Even after living through that, I still decided to share my story in hopes of helping readers realize a three of the most things about life.

First, you absolutely need to have courage. I am a living testament to the fact that life can come crashing completely down, but we have the uncanny ability to go on with life and somehow figure it out. Tragedy and bad luck has humbled me throughout my life, and to this day I have no explanation for where I found the courage to keep going. It was just always there. We all have it in us—don't let yourself resign to the bad out there so easily. Realize that we only have one life, so give yourself the courage to live it the way you want to.

The second, most important trait one must possess to navigate through life is a good sense of humor. I have learned first-hand that humor saves lives—it absolutely saved mine. The ability to laugh through tears is what got me through the moments of fear, devastation, and uncertainty. I am not saying that you have to laugh at everything and mask your sadness. No! It's okay to be sad, and it's okay to cry. In fact, it's healthy for you. Without understanding the tragedy in your life, you'll never come to appreciate all the good. And the third, final life lesson that you need to accept is this: Life Goes On. It's that simple. No matter what happens from one day to the next, there is one thing that is for sure—life will keep going.

So remember, live it the way you want, laugh along the way, and remember that with, or without you, life will keep on moving forward. Move in its direction with positivity and you'll be just fine.

207